THE CURATED TABLE

Recipes and Styling for the Perfect Meal

GINGKO PRESS

The Curated Table

Recipes and Styling for the Perfect Meal

First Published in the USA and in Europe by
Gingko Press by arrangement with
Sandu Publishing Co., Ltd.

GINGKO PRESS

Gingko Press, Inc.
2332 Fourth Street, Suite E
Berkeley, CA 94710 USA
Tel: (510) 898 1195
Fax: (510) 898 1196
Email: books@gingkopress.com
www.gingkopress.com

Gingko Press Verlags GmbH
Schulterblatt 58
D-20357 Hamburg / Germany
Tel. +49 (0)40-291425
Fax +49 (0)40-291055
Email: gingkopress@t-online.de

ISBN 978-1-58423-685-6

SANDU PUBLISHING ⊜ | 360°

Sponsored by Design 360°–
Concept & Design Magazine

Edited and produced by
Sandu Publishing Co., Ltd.

Publisher: Sandu Publishing Co., Ltd.
Chief Editor: Wang Shaoqiang
Executive Editor: Wang Naidan
Copy Editor: Jason Buchholz
Design Director: Wang Shaoqiang
Designers: Huang Zhiyi, Chen Yingqiao, Wu Yanting
Sales Managers: Niu Guanghui (China), Winnie Feng (International)

Photo on front cover by Carolin Strothe
Photo on back cover by Kathrin Salzwedel
Contents and index illustrations by Huang Zhiyi

info@sandupublishing.com
sales@sandupublishing.com
www.sandupublishing.com

Printed and bound in China

CONTENTS

PREFACE

By Samantha Woods

Food is inextricably bound with human existence; neither makes sense nor could exist without the other. In plain terms, our relationship with food is one of survival, yet to think of it so reductively makes far too little of the intimate bond we share with food. In reality the culture of food is far more spellbinding. Of us, food makes allies, companions and communities. We come of age over food; stake our reputation upon it; define our past by it. It might be unwitting on a daily basis but for every special occasion marked by a meal there's cause for wonder at the intrinsic magic between good food and humankind.

Unlike language, religion or history, there is a sense of universality to food. By all means, the cuisine of a place renders it distinct but the rituals surrounding preparation, inheritance and experience are in many ways interchangeable. All of humanity marks its time by daily meals; we all associate memories with food and everyone socializes over the dining table.

Sharing a meal is an intimate experience. It invites pause and connects us momentarily to all of our senses. If we allow it, chaos and distraction can fall away over the dining table, and the meal can instead center our focus upon pleasure and kept company. How often we are restored by a family meal, made content after dining with friends, unburdened, enlightened or impassioned by dinner-time conversation.

The ritual of dining does take a measure of devotion, because nowadays the lure of convenience is all-too seductive. Our lives make for such busy affairs and so any means of time-saving can be wickedly appealing. By forsaking our plate, though, we do ourselves a disservice; we sacrifice our health, disconnect from our environment and neglect our social nature.

As we begin to slow ourselves down and live with more considered intention, the curated table is a place for that existence to take root. It is a practice irrespective of means and free of expectation. Rather, in becoming curators, we simply invite more occasions for ourselves and others to gather in reverence of good food and genuine connection.

In the curated table a place is made; it might be temporary but it still entertains human occupation for a brief window of time. It doesn't require extravagance or opulence—in fact, there's often beauty in the prosaic. It merely takes consideration. It's not a particularly new notion, of course; every day all over the world people make places for themselves at their tables. Even the simple act of laying cutlery and napkins has a measure of thoughtfulness about it. Yet by thinking of the sometimes unnoticed things—the materials, the palette, the provenance—we heighten what joy there is in the experience.

As we come to appreciate what delight there is in an assembled table— be it crowded, coupled or solitary—no longer is the kitchen such a place of uncertainty. We are learning with increasing interest to reconnect with our heritage, community and seasonality through food.

Human hands make food enchanting. It is an artist's medium just as much as a fundamental necessity. By simple esteem of ingredients, tradition and slow preparation we can imbue our plate with an unspoken quality, an energy that passes from cook to diner. Good food might not always be convenient but it can be simple and earnest. Imperfection isn't something to loathe—even a weepy meringue in its creation attests to devotion. We need only learn to remain inquisitive, find guidance, follow recipes and experiment.

In the pages that follow, you will find such encouragement. Culinary stories are woven through what is essentially a guide to table scenery and homemade food. The narrative is poetic yet practical and it makes what might seem arduous into a novel pursuit. We who grace the pages are no different from any reader; coming from diverse backgrounds often unrelated to food we are affected by all the same time pressures, insecurities and sometimes failed meals.

As a collective we understand the profound magic that can be found in a curated table, though. We've crafted rituals, lifestyles and businesses in celebration of food and it is with such pleasure that we share our insights. At the end, come seek us out—we exist with even more animation off-paper and love nothing more than new companions. For now, though, let the coming revelation wash over you; let it instruct you and inspire you. Be open to transformation and enlightenment; be slow and intentional and realize that this is as much about your own table as it is ours.

"In the curated table a place is made; it might be temporary but it still entertains human occupation for a brief window of time. It doesn't require extravagance or opulence—in fact, there's often beauty in the prosaic. It merely takes consideration."

—Samantha Woods

Beata Lubas

Blog/ **Bea's Cookbook**

"Food connects and brings us all together. It doesn't only feed our body, but it also feeds our soul."

Beata Lubas is the food photographer, stylist and writer behind the blog "Bea's Cookbook." She fills her blog with homey food and conveys a positive life attitude. Born and raised in Poland, she moved to England in 2006, where she discovered that food photography is her lifelong passion.

The Smiling Foodie

Your portrait conveys a lot about your characteristics. For those who have lingered a moment on Beata Lubas's blog, "Bea's Cookbook," it is easy to be enthralled by her warm smile, abundant emotions behind her photos and her positive life attitude.

Beata grew up in a picturesque town in southwestern Poland. Although she was not a frequent visitor of the kitchen, living close to nature cultivated her appreciation of fresh produce and its natural taste. Determined to go on a self-discovery journey, she moved from Poland to England with her husband in 2006. She packed her suitcase full of longing and her constant love for delicious food. After she had been in her new country for a period of time, she found that something was missing: the flavor of her hometown. "When I moved away from home, I realized that I always took great food for granted. Nothing I prepared or got from the shop tasted like the meals prepared by my family. And that's how my adventure with cooking started," Beata recalls.

Missing her family home was the reason that Beata started cooking. Her upbringing in Poland and her love of nature and Polish culture deeply influence her culinary philosophy. As a firm advocate of cooking with raw, seasonal and fresh ingredients, she loves cooking from scratch and growing her own fruit and vegetables.

Among all the food she has cooked, there is one that always arouses sentiment—traditional Polish apple pie. When she feels homesick, Beata bakes the apple pie in the way her mother made it. Its taste brings her back to her home country, to the Polish market shining with different kinds of apples, and to the apple tree in her parents' garden.

Besides food, Polish table culture also sowed a seed in her memory. Beata mentions that, in Poland, a lot of events happen around the table, whether it's a big weekend breakfast with the family, someone's birthday, anniversary, special celebration or occasional gathering with friends. "It wasn't a big surprise that the first thing my husband and I bought for our small house was in fact a big table that has ever since been the heart of our home."

Polish culture is imprinted on her, but it was going to England that started a new chapter in her life. England opened a new world of flavor for her, and she was obsessively cooking, collecting cookbooks. In the meantime, she bought her first DSLR camera and started documenting her photos and recipes on her blog, called "Bea's Cookbook."

"I remember the first time when I took a camera in my hands. It was really like one of those OMG! moments. I

felt like a whole new world just opened in front of me. I was dancing with happiness and I couldn't wait to learn more," Beata recalls.

With a camera in her hands, her subject is the food she makes. "I really believe that we first eat with our eyes, and how food looks really makes the meal even more special. Food is so much more than just a few ingredients mixing together." Beata talks about her perception of food photography. "I hope my photos will make people look at food from a different perspective, to maybe take time to cook something delicious, to sit around the table with those who matter to us the most, to make each meal a special celebration."

Looking back to this journey of food photography and blogging, Beata is grateful for all the possibilities she has been given and all the talented people she has encountered. She has held workshops where she shared experience in food photography and associated with like-minded people to explore food and its meaning for people. Talking about her plan for the future, she says she will always work on her craft to become a better photographer.

1. How do you describe your cooking style?

I'd say it's mainly simple, homey, comforting and full of flavor! If you saw my "flavor drawer" you'd know what I mean. Spices and herbs are the ingredients I love to play with.

2. When and how did your journey as a food blogger begin? Does it take a lot of time and effort?

I wanted to practice food photography and felt that committing to something like a blog would motivate me to try different food and learn how to photograph it. I was also inspired by amazing blogs that I came across. So many incredible people out there!

I am not going to lie—it's hard work, but if you love what you do, you don't really look at it that way. It takes a lot of time, but it also brings you an immeasurable amount of happiness and huge satisfaction.

3. Can you talk about the inspiration for your recipes?

The inspirations come from everywhere! Cookbooks, blogs, friends and family! I am always inspired by the seasons and food that is available around, because that's when it tastes its best. But nothing sparks my ideas for new recipes like traveling. That's when I feel all of my senses experience everything on a totally different level. And I really don't have to go too far—sometimes a day trip to a nearby city or town can turn into a great source of inspiration.

4. What elements do you think influence food styling and photography? Do you have favorite props? Why do you choose them?

I believe that our personalities are reflected in our work, so what you can see in my photographs is me. These emotions I want to reflect in my images are the very emotions I am attracted to, the ones that I am craving.

My photography is always influenced by the light around me, how it changes with the seasons and times of the day. I love to observe it and see how it affects the subject on my images. I do love to play with colors! This is also influenced by how the colors change around us in spring, summer, autumn and winter. Creativity for sure is a food for my soul.

I usually choose quite plain props that do not distract people's attention from food, but I do love rustic elements like vintage cutlery, because they always tell some kind of a story.

5. I feel like "smile" is a keyword for you—you have a prop that spells it out, and your smile in the portrait is so warm. So can I assume that, whether in your photos or in your blog, you wish to convey a positive life attitude?

I really hope that this positive vibe I carry in my heart is reflected in everything I do. I am so happy to hear that this is the impression you get.

If you ask me if I see the glass half-empty or half-full, I'll tell you that I am grateful that I have a glass. I believe that the world is a reflection of who we are. If we look at it with a positive attitude (and I know sometimes it is not easy!), we are able to notice magic and happiness around us and even more positivity comes back to us.

6. From associating with like-minded food bloggers and photographers, what do you think is the trend in home cooking?

There is so much "fake" food around, made with "dishonest" ingredients, that people started to appreciate the flavor and nourishment of home-cooked food. I have also noticed on social media that people cook from scratch more and more. I think these are some of the reasons why we all crave to eat with much more intention these days, and why we choose better-quality food, support local businesses, and why we prefer to cook at home and sit together at one table.

Apple Pie

» Ingredients

Pastry

· 2 cups (300 g) plain flour

· 1 ¾ sticks (200 g) butter, cold, chopped

· 2 tablespoons icing sugar

· 2 teaspoons of vanilla paste

· 1 egg yolk

· 2-4 tablespoons of cold water (if necessary)

Apple filling

· 2.5 pounds (1.2 kg) apples, firm and hard

· Juice from half a lemon

· ⅔ cup (75 g) sugar

· 1 tablespoon butter, unsalted

· 2 teaspoons vanilla paste

· 1 ½ teaspoons cardamom

· 1 teaspoon cinnamon

· 1 tablespoon of cold water mixed with 1 tablespoon of potato flour

Also

· 1 egg, beaten, for brushing the pastry

· Coarse sugar for sprinkling on the pastry (optional)

» Method

1. For the pastry: put the flour, butter, and icing sugar in a bowl, and use your fingertips to rub the ingredients together until they resemble coarse breadcrumbs. Add the vanilla paste and the egg yolk and work into the pastry to combine, until you have a smooth dough. If the pastry feels too dry, add cold water starting from 1 tablespoon. If the pastry feels too moist add some more flour. Divide the pastry into two parts, one slightly bigger (it will be the bottom of the pie). Wrap them both in cling film and chill for at least 30 minutes.

2. On a lightly floured surface, roll out the bigger part of the pastry to fit a 9" (23 cm) tart/pie tin. Line the tin, trimming the edges. (You can save the trimmings with the rest of the pastry and use it for the top of the pie). Prick the pastry with fork and refrigerate for another 30 minutes.

3. In the meantime prepare the filling. Squeeze the lemon juice and pour it into a larger pot. Peel the apples, remove the cores, chop them and mix with the lemon juice. Add the sugar, butter, vanilla paste, cardamom and cinnamon and cook on a medium heat for around 15 minutes until the apples are caramelized. Let the apple mixture cool down. Mix 1 tablespoon of cold water with 1 tablespoon of potato flour and pour over the apple mixture. Mix well.

4. Preheat the oven to 375°F (190°C). Take the tin lined with pastry out of the fridge and fill it with apple pieces. Roll out a smaller part, cut into strips and arrange them on the top of the pie. Brush each strip with a beaten egg and sprinkle with coarse sugar if desired. Bake for 40-45 minutes until pastry is crisp and golden.

Waffles

Makes 5–6

» Ingredients

Dry ingredients

· 1 cup (150 g) plain bread flour

· 1 teaspoon dry yeast

· 1 teaspoon sugar

· ¼ teaspoon baking powder

· ¼ teaspoon cardamom

· ½ teaspoon cinnamon

Wet ingredients

· 13.5 ounces (250 ml) milk

· 3 ½ tablespoons (50 g) butter

· 1 egg

» Method

1. Sift the flour and mix all the dry ingredients together. Warm up the milk but don't heat it up too much. You can test it with the cooking thermometer—it should have a temperature of around 104°F (40°C). Add the butter and mix it with the spoon until it melts completely, then add the egg and whisk until smooth. Add the milk mixture to the dry ingredients and whisk until smooth.

2. Leave the batter to rest for 1 hour.

3. Heat the waffle maker, pour the batter mixture onto it and cook until golden and crisp with the instructions on your device.

4. Serve warm with your favorite toppings.

Katie Brigstock &
Safia Shakarchi

Brand/ **Cook & Baker**

"Eating is an immersive experience, and we like to make that shine."

Katie and Safia are two best friends who share the same passion for food. They met in the foodie Spanish capital Madrid and later established their own brand, Cook & Baker (Katie is the cook, and Safia is the baker). Starting with travel-inspired supper clubs, the creative duo have more exciting plans on the road.

Celebrating the Eating Ritual around a Dining Table

Foodie friends are not rare. But few of them would call each other a "foodie soulmate" and start a business together. Safia Shakarchi and Katie Brigstock are two of those people. The friends have much in common, from their early experiences to their intrinsic love of bringing people together over a simple feast.

Both Safia and Katie developed interests in food in childhood. In Katie's home, she was a master in creating a mess in the kitchen, and when she got older, the TV cookery shows of "Ready Steady Cook" and "MasterChef" became her fascination. Safia, on the other hand, was drawn to the sweet food made by her grandmother and learned how to make typical Middle Eastern desserts, such as *mahalabi*, a lovely and fragrant rosewater and cardamom pudding, which is still one of her favorites.

Throughout the years from high school to university, both of them had the experiences of writing food blogs, doing internships at food magazines, helping out in test kitchens and event planning. More importantly, they both loved hosting dinner parties, inviting friends and relatives over for a shared meal, which made them believe in food's power to bind people together.

Food waved its magic wand in 2016. Both Katie and Safia studied Spanish at university and they chose Madrid as their year-abroad destination. Through a mutual friend, they got to know each other and became friends immediately. The rest of the year witnessed their exploration of the beautiful cafés, restaurants and charming rooftops of Madrid, and since then, they have traveled to more than nineteen cities around the world.

When they came back to London in 2017, Katie enrolled in the Diploma at Leiths School of Food and Wine, and Safia, being attracted to the artistic side of food, began studying Patisserie at Le Cordon Bleu. Backed up by professional training and their ongoing desire, they decided it was the perfect time to start a project together. "We wanted to share our love for curating a beautiful table, for cooking up delicious food to share with our friends, and for design and creativity. We figured that the supper clubs were the perfect way to combine all three of our passions." Thus, Cook & Baker was born.

After preparation and planning, their first supper club kicked off at an industrial warehouse space in Hackney, in inner London. The Moroccan dishes served at the event and the styling were inspired by their dining experience in a restaurant in Marrakech, memorable not just for the mouth-watering date cake they ate, but also the overall atmosphere and the setting. "We were sitting

outdoors on the terrace at sunset, looking out onto the Marrakech skyline with festoon lighting draped above us. The black-and-white striped interior of the restaurant with its bamboo placemats and lampshades and its 'shabby chic' vibe made that evening all the more magical," they recall. It is those memorable and unique experiences of dining that they wish to re-create at their events.

Starting from Marrakech, and then moving to Ibiza and Berlin, and beyond, every supper club they hold is inspired by their travels and trips together. To create the immersive environments that reflect the specialty of that particular culture, Katie and Safia approach the styling in the same way that they approch their cooking and baking. In their Ibiza-inspired supper club, they decorated the space with beige colors, soft-tone props and macramé plant hangers, which remind people of the relaxing atmosphere of that beachy island. The travel-

inspired dishes, together with the finely decorated environment, make for an immersive, meaningful evening.

Over the years, Katie and Safia have been pleased to see the bonds and new connections that form over their tables. There are guests who come alone, but are the last ones to leave. Besides guests, they also establish working relationships with small businesses, whose products, such as homemade plates, add another story to the dish served.

In the future, Katie and Safia wish they could have a permanent Cook & Baker space to turn into a home for all their ideas and styling inspirations, holding workshops, supper clubs and retreats, hopefully with a yoga studio alongside for Katie to teach in and Safia's own bakery. It would be open for people to explore and join in the Cook & Baker community.

"There is no doubt that every journey through food begins with and is centered on what is on your plate. The quality of the ingredients, the combination of the flavors, and the way that they come together to create something far greater than the sum of those individual elements—that's what makes food so special."

1. How would you each describe your culinary philosophy?

K: Fresh, seasonal and something that you'd love to share with your friends. I'm not one for something overly complicated. My kind of cooking style revolves around the seasons and what I feel like making that day. I don't have much patience for following exact recipes (hence why I'm not the baker!), so my favorite type of cooking is where I can get hold of a few really spectacular fresh ingredients and center a dish around them. I think it's so important to celebrate local produce, and the difference in flavor and quality of produce that has been truly cared for and nurtured is outstanding.

S: Simple, comforting and definitely seasonal. I think baking is a matter of mastering the basics though— once you've got that foundation, you can play around, experiment with the seasons and find your own style. That's why I love following exact recipes. You begin to learn the role that each ingredient plays in a pastry or a cake, so that next time you can change it slightly to make something new. Sometimes it might end in total disaster, but other times you end up with something amazing, and that's what makes the process so enjoyable. I also believe that the way you bake has a lot to do with how you feel. It's funny—when I'm in a bad mood or I'm stressed out, my cakes often turn out

totally wrong. I've ended up with a lot of sunken cakes as a result (how poetic!). But when I am relaxed and I am loving what I'm doing, it turns out great. It's really about making something with love.

2. Recalling your first-ever supper club, were there exciting, surprising or nervous moments that stand out?

K&S: The moment we put tickets on sale! We had absolutely no idea what to expect, and the response was just amazing. We didn't at all expect to sell out, let alone so quickly. It was really humbling, and such an exciting time too.

We also vividly remember the moment that we put our first-ever long banquet table together. There's something so special about seeing all those chairs in line with their places set. It took almost six of us, and after almost having it set, we decided to move it all down a meter and had to re-align the whole thing! But it's that attention to detail that makes the final result so rewarding.

At each event, we also still address our guests around the table, and to this day we have to take a few breaths to let it all sink in and appreciate what we have created.

3. In regards to table setting and event styling, how do you determine the design feature of each event?

K&S: For us, the styling is such an important part of each event and it forms a key part in why we do what we do. Little details and touches can make such a difference to the feel and atmosphere of an evening—they help us make our guests feel at home and part of something special.

We like to think that the story behind each piece that we have sourced and styled adds another layer to the evening—from the hand-poured candles that we sourced from a family-run business, to candlesticks that we bought on our travels. Our events bring together people and makers who are passionate about what they do, including ourselves, and we think that really comes through in the experience of a Cook & Baker evening. We like to tell stories.

In the run-up to the event, we create mood and color boards, and we spend time researching different creatives and brands who fit the theme and image we are going for. Along the way we've also learnt our own little tricks too—we now often buy lengths of beautiful fabric and rip them into napkins ourselves.

When styling, we also often find less is more. We choose to source really beautiful pieces that speak for themselves and that make a statement on our tables. Above all, we aim for elegance and simplicity. We love muted and natural tones with occasional pops of color—nothing that stands out too much, but rather softness and subtlety. We want every element to complement the next and to come together to create a stunning, carefully considered and lovingly curated table.

4. Have you encountered problems or obstacles during the setting, styling or organizing of the event?

K&S: We're so lucky to have been surrounded by a wonderful community of talented individuals and young creatives who have helped us do that, and ensured that every little detail at our supper clubs is just as we imagined. From ceramicists to floral designers and other entrepreneurs, we've had the pleasure of working with some incredible people and featuring the different decorative elements that they create on our tables at each event.

Of course, starting a business is never a totally smooth ride, and we've definitely encountered our fair share of problems along the way! Sometimes we think we're totally crazy, taking on the jobs of about sixteen different people between just the two of us. It feels like we're organizing a wedding each month and working freelance alongside Cook & Baker means emails at 1 a.m., little sleep and charging around London in a car packed full to the brim. However, we wouldn't swap it for anything. To be honest, one of the hardest parts of it all is learning what suits you as a business and what doesn't, and being okay with saying no to some opportunities too. We've had to accept that we just can't do everything, even though we want to!

5. What kind of feeling do you expect your guests to have when they attend the supper clubs?

K&S: We want our guests to feel like they have come over to our home for dinner and spent an evening with friends, both old and new. At the same time, we want them to experience something unique, an environment that offers the opportunity to connect with other like-minded people and strike up a conversation with a stranger who might become a lifelong friend. It's important to us that they enjoy all that in a relaxed, beautiful and welcoming space.

We also like our guests to feel that our events are really personalized and that they are being spoiled—because everyone deserves to feel that way sometimes, from the welcome drinks that we serve, to the seating arrangement that we spend time carefully planning, to the individual gift bags that guests will always find on their seats. Our events might begin when our guests walk through the door, but we want the experience to last right up until they get home and stay with them as a lovely and fond memory.

Elderflower, Gooseberry & Pistachio Cake with Yogurt Cream

Makes 1 large bundt cake, or 24 mini bundts

» Ingredients

For the cake

- ¾ cup (190 g) baker's sugar
- 5 large eggs
- 1 teaspoon lemon zest
- ½ cup (120 ml) elderflower cordial
- ½ cup (120 ml) light olive oil
- 1 ⅔ cups (250 g) plain flour
- 2 teaspoons baking powder

For the drizzle

- 2 tablespoons (30 ml) water
- ½ cup (60 g) baker's sugar
- 4 tablespoons elderflower cordial
- Juice of half of a lemon

For the cream

- ⅘ cup (200 ml) double cream
- 1 teaspoon icing sugar
- ⅞ cup (200 g) cream cheese
- 2 tablespoons Greek yogurt

Gooseberry compote

- 2 cups (200 g) gooseberries
- ¼ cup (30 g) baker's sugar

To serve

Crushed pistachios

» Method

1. Preheat the oven to 360°F (180°C) and generously grease a large bundt or mini bundt tin with oil or cooking spray. Take care here so that the cake doesn't stick.

2. Begin by whisking the baker's sugar, eggs and lemon zest for 5 minutes until thick and slightly paler in color. Combine the olive oil and elderflower cordial in a jug and gradually add this to the egg mixture, being careful not to overmix. Sift together the flour and baking powder and fold this gently into the wet ingredients in two batches.

3. Pour the batter into the prepared tin and bake in the oven for 35 to 40 minutes if making a large cake, or 15 minutes if making mini bundt cakes. The cakes will be ready when a skewer inserted comes out clean.

4. While the cake is in the oven, make the syrup. Warm the water and sugar gently in a small saucepan until the sugar has completely dissolved. Remove from the heat and stir in the elderflower cordial and lemon juice.

5. Once the cakes have come out the oven, pierce all over with a skewer and brush generously with the syrup using a pastry brush. Leave to cool in the tin for 10 minutes before turning out onto a wire rack to cool completely.

6. To make the compote, place the gooseberries and baker's sugar into a small saucepan over a gentle heat for 10 to 15 minutes, or until the gooseberries begin to soften but still hold their shape. Drain if necessary, and set to one side until ready to serve.

7. When ready to serve, whip the cream together with the icing sugar to form soft peaks. Gradually whisk in the cream cheese, followed by the Greek yogurt—the cream should hold well. Sprinkle some pistachios onto the plate and top with a spoonful of gooseberry compote. Place a slice or mini bundt cake on top of the compote, and pipe or spoon a few dollops of cream around the edge. Finish with a few fresh gooseberries if you have them.

Grilled Peach and Burrata Summer Salad

Serves 4

» Ingredients

For the salad

· 4 medium-ripe peaches (sweet and ripe but firm enough to grill)
· 2 tablespoons oil (use flavorless oil like rapeseed or sunflower oil)
· 2 cups (200 g) burrata
· ¾ cup (100 g) walnuts
· 5 cups (250 g) chicory or endive
· 3 cups (100 g) watercress
· ¼ cup (50 g) spinach
· Micro herbs to garnish (Katie suggests red amaranth)

For the dressing

· 4 tablespoons olive oil
· 2 tablespoons honey
· 2 tablespoons balsamic vinegar
· 1 to 2 tablespoons lemon juice
· Sea salt
· Black pepper

» Method

1. Place a griddle pan over a high heat. Cut the peaches in half, remove the stones and brush the flesh with oil.

2. Once the griddle pan is hot, grill the peaches, flesh side down, for 2 to 3 minutes until they begin to caramelize and take on color. Remove from the grill and place to one side. Cut each peach half into 3 segments.

3. Wash and prepare the chicory by cutting off the hard stalks and peeling apart the individual leaves. Wash the watercress and spinach and mix together.

4. Crush the walnuts into small pieces with a knife. You can toast these lightly for a few minutes in a frying pan to bring out more of the nutty flavor and release the oil.

5. To make the dressing, mix the olive oil, honey and balsamic vinegar with a fork until well-combined. Season with salt, pepper and lemon juice to taste.

6. To assemble the salad, distribute the chicory leaves between the 4 plates. Top with a handful of spinach and watercress. With your hands, tear the burrata into small chunks and scatter over the plates. Top with the grilled peaches and crushed walnuts and drizzle over the dressing.

Samantha Woods

Blog/ **The Botanical Kitchen**

"Good food is rarely convenient, but it needn't be extravagant either; simplicity can yield the most savored meals."

Samantha Woods is the Australian creative behind the food blog "The Botanical Kitchen," where she writes poetically, eats plant-based seasonal food and craves a slow, genuine existence. Currently she resides in London.

Eating Botanically for a Caring and Considered Life

As a former architect, Australian creative Samantha Woods adores the idea of place-making. She transferred her love of designing places for human inhabitation to smaller scales: one's dining table. With fresh plant-based food, natural linen tablecloths, soft-tone tableware and a few green leafy plants, it could be said that Samantha's curated table scenery is clean yet rather enthralling, as if she is inviting you to take a seat and enjoy a serene moment.

Born in a suburban district of Australia, Samantha recalls she had a quiet upbringing filled with memories of carefree summers and family road trips. Her family food was characterized by convenience and domesticity. "Being Australian, our food culture is young, so for a time I lamented the absence of an inherited culinary lineage," Samantha says. "That was at a time I longed for foreign experiences though, nowadays I do realize the magic and freedom of Australia's burgeoning food scenes."

She accomplished both her Bachelor's and Master's degrees in architecture and worked as an architect for several years. It was in her early twenties when she began to feel discontent. Her unbridled imagination and ever-changing ideas called for a new means of unleashing creativity. It was around this time, she came to have her own kitchen, and her obsession with cooking started to grow tremendously. "The process of preparing food gave me a single point of concentration. It engaged my hands and quieted my mind. The kitchen became a place where the world would fall away," says Samantha.

In early 2016, she started her blog "The Botanical Kitchen" to document her "botanically minded" thoughts and recipes. She likes to cook simple plant-based food using fresh local produce. Over time, she has gradually perfected her recipes, infusing them with more detail and attention—beyond the main ingredients and cooking methods, Samantha has added seasonal ingredients and produce substitutions.

In her words, one can sense a discontentment with the fast pace of modern life and she herself craves more of a considered, genuine existence. She prefers handmade ceramic tableware over those mass-produced and she also encourages people to introduce slowness to their cookery.

"Cookery is one of the most obvious casualties in the pursuit of expediency. Poor-quality food and mindless consumption have become commonplace in daily life, so much so that people have lost touch with the true pleasures and rewards of slow preparations," says Samantha. By "slowness," she doesn't mean abandoning modern kitchen facilities, but rather she implores

more consideration of traditions, nourishment and provenance. "Let's face it, the world doesn't quiet down for such endeavors, rather it's we who need to learn the art of rejecting distraction in favor of the sustenance that comes from dining and gathering with care and consideration," she stresses.

In recognizing that others also long for simplicity amid the fast pace of modern life, Samantha has worked with a number of talented ladies, to give an otherwise virtual presence real-world substance. It began with a shared hosting of "the gathering table": small gatherings that would celebrate a simple feast and the kinship arising from a shared meal. These gatherings were held in a beautiful nursery on the Gold Coast where attendees could enjoy not only good food and warm company, but also a botanical surrounding. More recently her collaborations have expanded to include week-long

gatherings through Points North Workshops with Olivia Rubie, Linda Lomelino and Krissy O'Shea. These immersive experiences involve hours of planning, negotiating with local artisans and producers, and preparing food and table decorations; the occasions though are just as worthwhile for attendees as the hosts themselves.

In the autumn of 2017, Samantha made a bold and "mildly agonizing" decision: moving to London. Relocating halfway around the world, she admits there was indeed a period of time when she couldn't integrate with her new city and she yearned for the familiarity and stability of home. But the opportunities in this new place, which were previously unreachable, are worthy of striving for. "I'm determined to make the most of this occasion—there are grand adventures to be had before we return home," Samantha says.

1. From your photos of plants and fruits, I can tell that you are a nature lover. Is this the reason that you choose to keep a plant-based diet?

To be quite frank, I keep a plant-based diet mostly because meat doesn't marry well with my digestion. I had a lot of trouble before I began to decrease the amount of meat I ate and doing so has served me well ever since. I'm not stern with myself though and if I'm in a social setting where someone has gone to the trouble of preparing well-raised and ethically sourced meat, then I will appreciate the gesture and savor the meal. I simply choose to consume and celebrate nothing but plant-based dishes by my own hand.

Generally I think there's an imbalance with the modern diet; historically meat was always seen as a privilege, an indulgence reserved for moments of occasion. Today, however, it seems to adorn the plate of every daily meal and the consequences of such overconsumption are dire. A change in mentality is imperative. That doesn't necessarily have to equate to abstinence though; instead we should be supporting the farmers and producers who take an ethical and environmental stance.

2. You say that you love to cook with local produce. Where do you usually gather these ingredients?

Dwelling now in London I've come to realize just how fortunate I was in Australia in terms of the local produce. Our amenable climate meant that nearly every variety of fruit and vegetable was grown within a few hundred miles of home. My usual rounds included the farmers' market, self-serve dry goods store and artisan bakery. On occasion I might have also sought specialty products from a delicatessen or foreign grocer.

In the United Kingdom, sourcing fresh local produce is slightly more challenging though not unachievable. My first and foremost love will always be a marketplace: Borough Market in particular is a world where I can happily lose hours. Another slightly more practical means is to source local fresh produce through specialist curators. Fruit and vegetable boxes with locally grown contents are readily available to order online and are heaven-sent when I lack time.

3. In each recipe you share, you mark out the main ingredient, its climate, other potential ingredients and market variations. Could you talk about the development and research behind each recipe?

Recipe development can be rather absorbing. From that first moment of inspiration, it's rarely a simple or straightforward process. Personally, even the genesis of my ideas are unpredictable; inspiration might be owing to the plate of another, or to a particular flavor combination or to seasonality. Regardless, I often take a moment to note down the bones of a recipe before testing it at the table. On rare occasions, it might be perfect in the first instance, though more often than not it takes some amendments and another turn.

Seasonality dictates the availability of produce, obviously, so substitutions and variations are noted down for those in the face of similar shortages. Once happy, I'll finalize the recipe and research specific seasonality. For the main ingredients, I might also consult a flavor thesaurus for complementary additions, though more often than not I simply offer suggestions based on my own experiences.

4. How does your background in architecture and design influence your food styling?

As a professionally trained architect I love the ideas of architectural thinking—the idea of placemaking. The act of curating your silverware and crockery is at its heart a design process, one of thoughtful consideration or in some cases subconscious monotony. It doesn't require extravagance or opulence. In fact, there's often beauty in the prosaic; you need only invite conversation and company and the intention is fulfilled.

Interestingly, I think my food styling is less informed by my architectural background, or perhaps it's a subconscious influence. When composing dishes I tend to work more from a place of intuition. Naturally I understand rules of proportion and texture so they undoubtedly guide my hand but those aren't obvious thoughts that dictate my style. I tend to work through a process of trial and error.

Cashew & Miso Hummus

» Ingredients

- ½ cup (60 g) cashew nuts
- 1 ¼ cups (450 g) chickpeas, cooked
- ¼ cup (60 g) tahini
- ¼ cup (60 g) white miso
- ½ teaspoon chili flakes
- 2 tablespoons rice wine vinegar
- 1 tablespoon honey
- 2 tablespoons extra virgin olive oil
- ¼ cup ice water
- Salt & pepper

Seasonal variations

- Spring: asparagus & green beans, toasted sesame seeds, shaved parmesan, white peach, pea shoots
- Summer: cucumber & strawberry, fresh chèvre, pistachio, sprouts
- Fall: roasted beets & grapes, smoked almonds, figs, mixed leaves
- Winter: roasted pumpkin & cauliflower, hazelnut dukkah, persimmon, mixed leaves

Samantha: I am ever in pursuit of that elusive gracefulness that comes with the art of gathering. Time is often a finite resource during moments of occasion and so preparations with a measure of ease are invaluable. This plate is just that—a composition that is basic yet fanciful. It's perfect for entertaining and is a cinch to construct.

» Method

1. Begin by blending all of the above ingredients in a high-speed blender until the hummus is smooth and creamy.

2. Spread the hummus upon a large serving plate and top with a selection of fresh seasonal produce.

Samantha's rendition includes:
Heirloom cherry tomatoes, halved
Cucumber, sliced
Watermelon radish, sliced
Corn kernels
Cherries, pitted and halved
Blackberries
Blueberries
Pomegranate
Amaranth leaves
Borage flowers
Salt & Pepper

3. Serve immediately with seeded bread.

Midsummer Greens with Mint Chutney & Burrata

» Ingredients

· 1 fresh burrata

· 4 cups (250 g) cannellini beans, soaked and cooked

· 1 cup (155 g) of fresh or frozen edamame beans, cooked and shelled

· 1 ⅓ cups (150 g) of fresh peas, shelled and cooked

· 2 cups of mint leaves, firmly packed, stems discarded

· 3 medjool dates, if dry or hard, soak in hot water for a few minutes first

· 1 teaspoon of minced ginger

· 1 teaspoon of red chili flakes

· 5 teaspoons (25 ml) of lime juice

· 2 tablespoons of extra virgin olive oil

· Sea salt and freshly ground black pepper

To serve

· Rye bread, sliced and toasted

Market variations

· Asparagus / broad beans / fresh pesto / labneh

· Charred radishes / grilled corn / fresh parsley / lemon

· Fresh strawberries / lime / chopped pistachios / chèvre

» Method

1. To begin, prepare the mint chutney. Wash and dry the mint leaves.

2. In a high-speed blender mince the ginger, chili flakes and lime juice. Add the dates, mint and olive oil and continue to pulse until well-combined. Samantha likes to leave a little texture but you can also blend it until smooth.

3. Season the chutney with salt and pepper to taste.

4. Meanwhile prepare the plate. Dry cannellini beans have a much nicer bite so where possible use these by soaking overnight and boiling for 45 to 90 minutes (this will depend on the age of the beans), check intermittently to see whether they're tender.

5. Fresh edamame beans and fresh peas also make this dish extra special so use them if you can. Samantha appreciates that edamame can be exceptionally difficult to find fresh so simply find the best-quality frozen otherwise (frozen edamame in their shells trump those pre-popped too).

6. Once you have all your beans and peas prepared, in a large bowl fold through the mint chutney.

7. Plate your burrata on a large serving dish and then spoon over the bean medley. Season with a touch more salt and pepper and then serve with sliced rye bread.

Carolin Strothe

Blog / **Frau Herzblut**

"For everything I do,
I do it with my heart and soul."

Carolin Strothe is a freelance food photographer, food stylist, art director and cookbook author based in Hannover, in northern Germany. Her passion for food is showcased on her blog "Frau Herzblut" in the form of fine bakery art and delicious vegetarian food, paired with a pinch of vintage charm, love of detail and natural elements.

To Food with Heart and Soul

The color purple is often associated with magic and royalty. With finely toned purple colors, the food photos of Carolin Strothe have an irresistible charm, alluring her readers to look at her carefully curated table, which is laden with vibrant food, delicate cutlery and treasures from nature.

When Carolin was a little girl, her parents' and grandparents' gardens were her wonderland. One of her favorite things to do was picking berries and apples in the garden and hunting for nature's treasures. With the fruit and vegetables from the family's own garden, her mom prepared many typical seasonal German dishes, like potato pancakes with applesauce, meatloaf with gravy, potatoes and steamed vegetables, and chicken fricassee with rice and asparagus. Complementary to these German dishes, her mom was also good at making Italian dishes and showed eight-year-old Carolin how to make tomato sauce. Since then, pasta dishes have been Carolin's favorite.

After her secondary school, Carolin undertook a three-year apprenticeship as a professional photographer and studied communication design at the University of Applied Sciences and Arts of Hannover. She later worked for a couple of design and advertising agencies, realizing food photography, editorial and corporate design projects.

Along with her professional career, her passion for baking and cooking grows day by day. She not only learns from her mother and adapts traditional recipes from her grandmother, but also enthusiastically tries recipes from magazines and books. Her childhood memories cultivate her appreciation of fresh produce and inspire her to cook with local, seasonal and organic ingredients. "During the week, I cook rather simple but also quick dishes with a special twist. On the weekend, I love to cook long and lavishly. So I produce lots of food by myself like sourdough, bread and coconut yogurt. To eat lots of vegetables and fruit is very important to me," says Carolin.

Besides food, Carolin also puts great emphasis on the styling of the table scene. Every detail is finely adjusted because she thinks it is the details that make the essential difference and help a picture stand out from the crowd.

Nowadays, Carolin works in her own studio, "tiger & leo," which she founded with her husband in 2009. She works as art director, photographer and food stylist, which allows her to combine all of her passions and work creatively. When she is not cooking and handling projects, she loves swing dance (Lindy Hop and Balboa), listening to swing music from the 1930s to the 1950s, and engaging in swing-era design and fashion. Visiting the farmers' market with her vintage bike is also her favorite thing to do during the weekend.

1. Who has had the deepest influence on your culinary journey?

Alfred Biolek, a German amateur TV chef. In the 1990s he had an extraordinary cooking show, where he invited celebrities to cook together with him. Gennaro Contaldo, who practically taught me everything about Italian cuisine, and Jamie Oliver, "The Naked Chef"—I'm so happy that I've met Jamie several times. I love his passion and that he gives each dish a special twist. It's such an honor to have Jamie as our godfather for our new book "Einfach natürlich backen" (DK Verlag).

2. How did you practice and improve your baking and cooking skills?

I learned to cook and bake from my mother and grandmother Ami. In addition, I have always loved trying recipes from magazines and books. I learned a lot by trying. It's also helpful if you learn which food pairings fit together well and to always keep your eyes and ears open for new influences and tastes.

3. We are very impressed by your skillful food styling and table setting. Would you like to talk about what elements you consider when experimenting with food styling?

When it comes to food styling, I always try to work with clear shapes, color contrasts and interesting textures. In addition, it's important to me that the styling looks natural, attractive and easy.

4. From your photos and your blog, we can tell that you love vintage fashion. Why are you so fascinated with vintage style?

My father is a third-generation master tailor for men and my mother is a master tailor for ladies. The interest in fashion came to me in the cradle, because my mother also sewed a lot of clothes for me. I particularly love the aesthetics and elegance of the swing era of the late 1930s through the early 1950s. In those days, it was just a matter of putting your hair in waves and wearing a tasteful outfit with matching accessories. In addition, I love swing music and like to dance the Lindy Hop or Balboa, with the right look!

5. Where did your love of swing come from?

When I was eight years old I loved rock-and-roll-dancing to Elvis Presley music with my dad. I also liked swing music at that time. But I got really excited about the Lindy Hop in 2009 when we celebrated New Year's Eve in Berlin. There, I saw a Lindy Hopper live for the first time. After that, my husband and I did our first swing dance class and since then we have loved it. My husband has been collecting records for eighteen years and also deejays, so of course swing records were added to our collection. Together we deejay at swing events.

The best thing about the Lindy Hop is that after just one dance (even after a stressful day), you can smile all over your face. It is a very free dance that embodies "pure lust for life." Just like Frankie Manning, the ambassador of swing, said: "I've never seen a Lindy Hopper who wasn't smiling. It's a happy dance. It makes you feel good."

Beet Ravioli with Spinach and Goat Cheese

Serves 4

» Ingredients

For the dough

· 1 cup (130 g) spelt flour (type 630)
· 4 tablespoons (30 g) organic beet powder
· ¼ cup (50 g) fine semolina
· 1 pinch of salt
· 2 large organic eggs

For the filling

· 1 ½ cups (370 g) goat's-milk cream cheese or ricotta
· A small handful (50 g) fresh baby leaf spinach
· 2 tablespoons fresh oregano
· 2 teaspoons lemon juice
· ½ tablespoon zest of an organic lemon, finely grated
· 2 tablespoons fine semolina
· ½ cup (50 g) organic cheese or Pecorino, finely grated
· Freshly grated nutmeg
· Salt
· Freshly ground black pepper

To serve

· 4 cups (500 g) mixed wild mushrooms (chanterelle, porcini, oyster mushrooms, shiitake mushrooms)
· 1 garlic clove, finely chopped
· 2 tablespoons olive oil
· Juice of a quarter of organic lemon
· Zest of half an organic lemon
· Salt
· Black pepper
· Chili flakes
· A few branches of lemon thyme
· A small bunch of fresh marjoram

» Method

1. Mix spelt flour, beet powder, semolina and salt in a bowl or on the clean work surface, and make a well in the middle. Break the eggs and start to mix the eggs with a fork, then stir in gradually more and more of the flour mixture until it's mixed together. If the dough is solid, go on kneading with hands. Dust the work surface with a little flour. Continue kneading and stretching the dough for about 10 minutes, until it's smooth and soft. Pat into a ball, wrap into cling film and leave to rest 30-60 minutes in the refrigerator, or until needed.

2. Blend goat cheese, baby leaf spinach, oregano, lemon juice and lemon zest to a fine paste. Add the semolina and the cheese. Season with nutmeg, salt and pepper. Roll out the pasta dough very thin using a pasta machine. Fill the ravioli and either shape them freehand or cut them with a ravioli wheel or use a ravioli mold.

3. Carefully clean the mushrooms with a mushroom brush and cut into bite-size pieces.
Heat a grill pan. Grill the mushrooms in little portions, one after the other.

4. Meanwhile, heat abundant salted water and let the ravioli simmer in the water for about 3 to 4 minutes until *al dente*, when they float to the top.

5. In a bowl, mix the mushrooms with the garlic, the olive oil and lemon juice and zest. Season with salt, pepper and chili flakes and add the thyme leaves. Mix the mushroom mixture with the ravioli. Serve on plates and sprinkle with marjoram leaves.

Blackberry Charlotte

Serves 4–6

Tips:
You can substitute 6 sheets of
gelatin with 1 teaspoon agar-agar.

» Ingredients

*For one Charlotte (approx. 6" or
16 cm)*
- · 6 organic gelatine leaves
- · 2 cups (300 g) deep-frozen
  blackberries (defrosted)
- · 1 ½ cups (350 g) organic yogurt
- · ⅓ cup (80 g) muscovado sugar
- · 1 teaspoon vanilla, ground
- · 1 teaspoon rose water
- · 2 teaspoons lemon juice
- · ½ cup (100 ml) cream
- · 13 Biscuits rose de Reims
  (sponge fingers)

To decorate
- · 2 cups (300 g) fresh blackberries
  and raspberries
- · Edible flowers

» Method

1. Set a cake ring to 6" (16 cm) diameter and place on a suitable plate. In a separate bowl, leave the gelatine to soak in ice-cold water.

2. Puree the blackberries in your food processor. Mix pureed blackberries, yogurt, muscovado sugar, vanilla, rose water and lemon juice until well-combined.

3. Whisk ⅓ cup (70 ml) of the cream separately until stiff and place in the fridge. In a saucepan, gently heat the remaining cream. Squeeze out the excess water from the gelatine leaves and add it to the warm cream. Stir until the gelatine has completely dissolved.

4. Add the yogurt mixture spoon-by-spoon to the lukewarm gelatine and stir very gently with a spatula or large spoon until completely combined. Then, carefully fold in the cream. Place the mixture in the fridge and give it another stir every 15 minutes. You want the jelly to be almost set but still liquid.

5. Straighten the sponge fingers with a sharp knife on a short side to make them stand better and place them inside your cake ring. Carefully, fill in the blackberry yogurt cream. Smooth the surface and let it rest in the fridge for 4 to 6 hours or overnight.

6. Before serving, remove the cake ring and decorate with the fresh berries.

Maggie Zhu

"My culinary philosophy is to try to make a dish as healthy as possible when I can, but I don't mind a bit of sugar and fat here and there to maintain the great taste."

Originally from China, Maggie Zhu is now an Austin-based writer, recipe developer, and photographer of the food blog "Omnivore's Cookbook." Her wish is to bring real-deal Chinese flavors to Western readers.

Introducing Eastern Flavor to the Western Kitchen

It goes beyond doubt that Chinese food is renowned around the world. Anyone who has eaten authentic Chinese food is familiar with the amazing balance of color, flavor, texture and presentation. As a born-and-raised Chinese, Maggie Zhu now lives in Austin, Texas, with her husband and runs the food blog "Omnivore's Cookbook," which aims to bring authentic Chinese food to Western diners.

To many beginners, cooking Chinese food seems intimidating because of the unfamiliar ingredients and cooking styles. So Maggie dedicates a lot of the space on her blog to help her readers source ingredients and to explain cooking techniques. Sometimes she tweaks a recipe into something very different to make the cooking easier and more approachable. She rarely asks her readers to deep-fry things, for example—she has a baked Three-Cup Chicken recipe, versus the traditional stir-fry approach. She also has recipes adapted for the slow cooker, such as braised ribs.

Maggie's extensive passion for cooking has its roots in a traditional Chinese family that cherishes food culture. The food they eat is northern Chinese home-style food that is simple and emphasizes vegetables. Some of the most common dishes included stir-fried greens (*choy sum*, Chinese broccoli, and cabbage) and braised meat (pork, beef, and lamb). This kind of food was on their dinner table almost every day, served with steamed rice or congee, with a simple soup on the side. On the weekends, family members would make water-boiled dumplings from scratch, and her mom would present the specialty dish that amazed everyone—boiled noodles with mouthwatering gravy.

Maggie's own culinary journey started during her graduate studies in Japan, when she cooked Japanese-style stir-fried sweet-and-sour chicken. Maggie still remembers it well. "I used cubed boneless skinless chicken thigh with an egg-and-flour batter, bell peppers, and white onion. The sauce was made from rice vinegar, soy sauce, and sugar. I used a beat-up nonstick skillet handed down from alumni on top of a gas stove." Maggie said although the result wouldn't be up to her current standards, it was the most complicated dish she had made since moving to Japan, and so she was more than satisfied.

Like many have found, living in a foreign country triggered Maggie's intent to improve her cooking skills. She started collecting simple recipes from Japanese cooking sites, taking recipe cards from the grocery store, and reading cookbooks, and tried to make dishes at home. These resources proved to be very helpful for Maggie—they taught her basic cooking skills and measuring and preparing ingredients.

After finishing her studies and going back to her hometown, Beijing, Maggie worked in a bank where the nine-to-five repetitive job made her feel miserable. Taking a friend's advice, Maggie started "Omnivore's Cookbook" in 2013 and has since dived into the world of blogging, where she still thrives.

In 2015, Maggie moved to the US with her husband, whom she met during her studies in Japan. She took a one-year online culinary course and earned a culinary degree, and now cooks in her Austin kitchen for her family. Because of Maggie's blog, the couple eat Chinese food very frequently, and the rest of the time she mostly makes very simple and healthy Western dishes with some Asian elements, such as salad, pan-fried fish, and baked vegetables.

Talking about her current life condition, Maggie feels quite content. "Austin is a small city, so life is quite peaceful and less overwhelming than it was in Beijing. We try to keep our lifestyle simple currently because we're both focusing on our careers. When we're not working, we travel as much as we can to see the world," Maggie says.

1. Do you have a favorite dish?

My favorite dish is still the most basic fried rice, made with leftover rice, eggs, green onion, and a pinch of salt. My mom doesn't like serving fried rice. She thinks it contains too much oil and is not very healthy, which makes it a special food for me, one that I constantly crave. I still make it often, even after moving to the US. It's one of those dishes that truly tastes like home.

2. We learned that you and your husband met in a Japanese teppanyaki restaurant. How would you describe this first encounter? Was it food that brought you together?

I'd say food and a common interest in foreign culture brought us together. I remember we were talking about topics like traveling in Egypt and culture shock the first time we met, and we hit it off immediately. It was definitely food that pulled us closer after that. I was so surprised that he invited me to his place and cooked for me during our early dating stage. He cooks so well! And he was very surprised that I could cook Western food. The first time I cooked for him, I made potato bacon salad and pasta bolognese. He told me the dishes reminded him of the taste of home.

3. What adjustments have you made in your recipes to make Chinese cooking more approachable for Westerners?

There are quite a few adjustments I make.

First, I try to be as accurate with measurements as possible, as opposed to the vague measurement usually given in a recipe. I use both metric and US units. Instead of saying "1 slice ginger, minced," I use "1 teaspoon minced ginger." I try to eliminate any ambiguity that might cause a reader to pause and think, "Hmmm, how big a slice is 'one slice?'"

Second, I try to pick cookware that Western people are familiar with. For example, I suggest using a Dutch oven to braise meat instead of a wok. I also recommend my readers use a nonstick skillet to make stir-fry instead of learning wok cooking, because the former is more practical on an electric stove, which is the most common setup.

Third, I incorporate cuts of meat and types of vegetables according to Western habits. I often replace chopped bone-in chicken with bone-in thighs, because people rarely want to deal with cutting up a chicken at home. I replace Chinese greens with more common vegetables in the supermarket, such as broccoli, to make grocery shopping easier.

Fourth, I advise ingredient substitutes when possible, such as soy sauce for light soy sauce, and dry sherry for Shaoxing wine, so people can make the dish if they don't have access to these ingredients.

4. Could you share one occasion when your food or preparation made a marvelous impression on your family and your friends? What's your tip for hosting a warm gathering?

There was one occasion that I considered the biggest win. I was hosting a dinner party plus cooking class for a family in the US. The main course was a northern Chinese gravy noodle. I had to use ingredients such as wood ear mushrooms and lily flowers, which are unknown and very strange to Western palates. They said the ingredients smelled like mud when I was rehydrating them. The mom whispered in my ear that her six-year-old son probably wouldn't eat the noodles and told me not to take any offense. She said he was a picky eater and prepared him some chicken and broccoli separately. When her son tried the kid-sized sample portion of noodles, he got really excited and asked for more. The mom was stunned. And of course, that dinner party was a blast and ended with smiles on everyone's faces.

My tip for hosting a gathering is to always listen to guests' requests when possible and pick out dishes with the demographics in mind. After living in the US for a while, I finally started to get an idea of popular food for different groups of people: Chinese immigrants vs. locals who've been to China vs. locals whose sole experience has been with American Chinese food. They have different preferences in Chinese food. I always try to select some dishes that most people will love, then I also prepare some of my favorite dishes to surprise them.

Black Pepper Steak

Serves 2

» Ingredients

1 pound (450 g) flank steak (or plate, or boneless short ribs, or sirloin), sliced against the grain into ¼" (5 mm)-thick pieces

Marinade
· 1 tablespoon soy sauce
· 1 tablespoon Shaoxing wine
· 1 tablespoon cornstarch

Sauce
· ½ cup beef broth (or chicken broth)
· 2 tablespoons soy sauce
· 2 tablespoons Shaoxing wine
· 1 teaspoon dark soy sauce
· 1 tablespoon cornstarch
· 2 teaspoons sugar
· 1 ½ teaspoons coarsely ground black pepper
· ⅛ teaspoon salt

Stir fry
· 2 tablespoons peanut oil (or vegetable oil)
· 1 teaspoon minced ginger
· 2 cloves garlic, minced
· ½ white onion, chopped
· 2 bell peppers, chopped

» Method

1. Combine steak, soy sauce, Shaoxing wine, and cornstarch in a medium-size bowl. Gently mix by hand until the beef is coated with a thin layer of the mixture. Marinate for 10 to 15 minutes.

2. Combine all the sauce ingredients in a small bowl. Mix well and set aside.

3. Cut the aromatics and vegetables. Add the ginger and garlic to a small bowl. Add the onion and all the chopped pepper to another bowl.

4. Heat 1 tablespoon of oil in a nonstick skillet (or a wok) over medium-high heat. When oil is hot, add the steak. Immediately spread the beef into a single layer using a pair of tongs or chopsticks. Sear for 30 seconds or so, until the bottom is lightly browned. Flip the beef with a spatula, until both sides are brown but still a bit pink inside. Turn to the lowest heat and remove the skillet from the stove. Transfer the beef to a plate and set aside.

5. Add the remaining tablespoon of oil into the same skillet and turn to medium heat. Add the ginger and garlic. Give it a quick stir until fragrant. Add the white onion and peppers. Stir and cook for 20 seconds.

6. Stir the sauce mixture until the cornstarch is dissolved completely, and pour it into the skillet. Stir with a spatula immediately and cook until the sauce thickens enough to coat the back of a spoon, a few seconds. Add back the cooked beef. Quickly stir a few times to coat everything with the sauce. Turn off heat and remove the skillet from the stove. Immediately transfer everything to a big plate so the ingredients won't keep cooking in the hot skillet.

7. Serve hot with steamed rice or on top of boiled noodles.

Vegetarian Pumpkin Soup

Serves 4–6

» Ingredients

· 4 cups cooked kabocha squash, peeled (or 2 15-ounce cans of pumpkin puree) (see note below)
· 1 tablespoon olive oil
· 1 small white onion, minced
· 1 big slice ginger, coarsely chopped
· 2 cloves garlic, coarsely chopped
· Pinch of sea salt
· 1 tablespoon curry powder
· 4 cups vegetable broth
· (Optional) coconut milk, chopped parsley, crushed red pepper and/or pumpkin seeds for garnish

Note:

Besides kabocha squash, you can use butternut squash, acorn squash, or pumpkin. If using pumpkin, you might want to add a bit of sugar to sweeten the soup.

» Method

1. Heat oil in a 3-quart Dutch oven (or pot) over medium heat until warm. Add onion, ginger, garlic, and a pinch of salt. Cook over medium-low heat and stir until the onion turns pale yellow, 10 minutes or so.

2. Add the curry powder. Stir and cook until the ingredients are evenly coated, 20 to 30 seconds.

3. Add the vegetable broth. Scrape the pan with a wooden spatula to release all the brown bits. Add the cooked pumpkin. Bring to a boil.

4. Transfer everything into a blender, leave the top plug of the blender open to let out the steam, and mix until the soup turns to a smooth texture. Alternatively, you can use a hand blender to mix the soup in the pot.

5. Transfer the soup into serving bowls. Garnish with coconut milk, parsley, crushed red pepper and pumpkin seeds (if using). Serve hot.

Agnes Gällhagen

Blog/ **Cashew Kitchen**

"I want my life to be rich and dynamic, where food is a source for abundance and joy."

Agnes Gällhagen is a food stylist, food photographer and recipe developer based in Sweden. She has a mixed educational background in art and human ecology. Besides being a total foodie, she enjoys shoegaze music, science fiction movies and novels, and early mornings.

Embrace the Imperfection

Cashews, which originated in Brazil, are chewy nuts rich in minerals and proteins. If consumed in the appropriate amount, they have incredible health benefits, including preventing heart disease, brightening the hair and helping digestion.

With her blog "Cashew Kitchen" Swedish food blogger Agnes Gällhagen has an indissoluble bond with this cute little nut. Because of her sensitive blood sugar, cashews are the most common type of nuts she snacks on between meals. They can also be used in a myriad of creative ways in the vegan kitchen: to make creamy sauces, ice cream or delicious nut butter.

Agnes grew up partly in central Stockholm and partly in a suburb close to a big nature reserve. She became a vegetarian at the age of fourteen and she started making vegetarian dishes, such as curries and hummus, by herself at home. While her interest in cooking was growing, she was also struggling with body image, which led her to control her eating in an unhealthy way. She would replace butter and cheese in a sandwich with cucumber and tomato, and she didn't allow herself to eat snacks between meals.

This issue of disordered eating became more serious when she was in her early twenties. Guilty feelings arose when she missed a workout session or indulged with candy in weak moments. In order to combat the guilty feelings, she tried to eat as healthy as she could, trying to cultivate the perfect body in a quest to be flawless. However, the controlled and restricted eating had a negative effect on her physical and mental health. Stomach issues, chronic throat aches, anxiety and pressure constantly bothered her.

In 2014, after years of training in art school, Agnes changed direction and enrolled in the Human Ecology program at Gothenburg University. It was during this time when she started her first food blog. She was amazed how this platform could allow her to play around in the kitchen, create stunning imagery, and write about meaningful topics like the environment, creativity and holistic health. The creation process so fascinated her that she started reading more on cooking methods, plant-based food and recipes through blogs and books.

In the meantime, her disordered eating gradually subsided, not only because she learned more about food, but was also able to emerge from under the psychological burden of staying perfect. "I've had to completely shift my mindset around wellness," Agnes says, "to think about it as something that nourishes both my body and my soul. Sometimes, wellness is not about eating the healthiest meal, but instead buying take-out because you're so tired that what you really need is to do nothing."

It was a gradual and winding process for her to let go of control and adopt a more accepting approach to food. "Now I eat plenty of nutrient-dense vegetables, fruits, grains and legumes, but I also eat cheese and eggs and licorice and chocolate. I drink wine and coffee," Agnes says. Sometimes when she still catches herself thinking about certain foods being "bad," she tries to act in the opposite way and fight against these fears.

In the spring of 2018, Agnes left her apartment in Stockholm to move to a house in Piteå, a small town in the north of Sweden. She has always dreamed of living in a beautiful house with her partner, of spending her weekends gardening and playing with the dog, and now that has all come into reality. Beyond that, she enjoys a bigger kitchen which can harbor more ingredients and provides more space for her to cook nourishing, home-style food. Although her life in Piteå is peaceful and quiet, Agnes is pondering a lot of exciting plans for the future, including writing a cookbook, generating more spiritual, inspiring lifestyle content for her blog's readers, and maintaining connection with her community.

1. What is your food philosophy now?

I don't want to live a life where food is a minefield I constantly have to navigate, where making one poor decision can result in a BOOM that throws me back to a place of self-doubt and fear. Now I try to think about what I can add in that's good for me, rather than what I should exclude. I explore food that intrigues me. I let hunger and cravings be my guide.

There's no perfect diet. It fluctuates, just like life does. I have guilty pleasures just like anybody else, and I don't try to hide them or restrict them. In fact, they enrich my life and make me feel worthy of being loved and feeling good in my own skin.

In my universe there's a time and place for all these things. Some nourish the soul, some the body, some both. Some things happen out of convenience and some out of mindfulness. I think about my body as strong, resilient and capable. It can handle all of these things. Some days I certainly don't feel like that, but then I remind myself: I am strong, I am resilient.

2. What tips would you give to those who have also struggled with their relationships with food?

If you struggle with food and feelings of anxiety or not being good enough, I want you to know that it is okay, and that you are not alone in your struggles. The difficulty you experience in dealing with these issues does not mean that you are weak or flawed.

I also want to say that you don't have to go through this process alone. For me it has helped tremendously talking to a professional about my anxiety, fears and controlling patterns. CBT (cognitive behavioral therapy) can be especially helpful as it provides concrete tools for dealing with anxious thoughts or feelings when they appear. It teaches us that we don't always have to act on our sudden fears but that it is possible to bear with them until they naturally decrease, when the body realizes the threat is over.

I would also recommend you let acceptance into your lives. By that I mean acceptance towards your own thoughts and feelings, which is something I'm working on myself a lot: to recognize my fears and uncomfortable thoughts and accept that they are there. I find that this often takes the power out of the emotion and makes it much easier to live with.

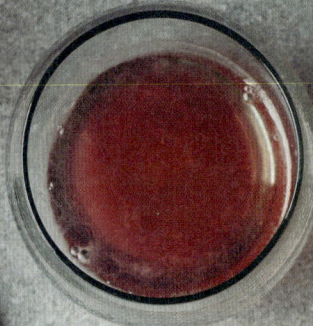

3. In terms of recipe development, how do you keep yourself inspired?

Most of the time I let my stomach decide. What do I crave right now? And what goes well with that? Hmmm, maybe something green for color and vibrancy. And something crunchy for texture. I let flavor combos, colors and textures guide me. It's a simultaneous process that is both artistic and pure craving.

Many recipes are born out of my everyday cooking, and stuff that catches my interest in the grocery store or the leftover bits and pieces from the crisp drawer. The best recipes always happen by accident, when I subconsciously let my gut feeling decide, only to realize, "Holy wow, this is delicious!"

4. What cutlery and props do you often use for food styling and photography?

I usually rotate a handful of favorite props. The props you see in my photos are the same ones I use privately. There's no need to keep beautiful bowls and cutlery stored away out of sight! Bring them out into the open and use them daily. That way we can truly appreciate their beauty and the craft that went into them.

Some favorite props that keep appearing in my pictures are my oxidized silver spoons (found cheap in flea markets), my handmade ceramic bowls, linen napkins and my old wooden desk. Most of the backdrops I use are either furniture from my home or old pieces of wood found at construction sites.

Sesame, Apricot & Mulberry Granola

Tips:

1. This recipe is gluten-free if you use gluten-free oats, and vegan if you choose maple syrup instead of honey.

2. The coconut tahini sauce makes for a pretty rad salted caramel sauce. Make extra and pour on ice cream! Perhaps go a little easy on the salt though, if you're planning to eat the sauce as-is.

Makes one large jar

» Ingredients

- 2 ¼ cups rolled oats (use gluten-free if you're sensitive)
- ⅓ cup sunflower seeds
- ½ cup pumpkin seeds
- ½ cup hazelnuts, roughly chopped
- ½ cup almonds, roughly chopped
- 2 tablespoons sesame seeds
- 2 teaspoons cinnamon
- 1 teaspoon ground and dried ginger
- ¾ teaspoon ground cardamom
- 8 organic unsulfured apricots, chopped
- ⅓ cup dried mulberries

Wet ingredients

- ⅓ cup coconut oil
- ¼ cup honey or maple syrup
- 2 tablespoons tahini
- A good pinch of vanilla powder
- ¼ teaspoon pink himalaya salt or sea salt

Agnes: I can never get enough of granola recipes! This one with sesame, apricot and mulberries feels like a cosy hug on a winter morning. It's simply a straight-up delicious combination of flavors and textures. Warm, spicy, crunchy, caramel-like, chewy.

» Method

1. Heat oven to 350°F (175°C).

2. Combine all dry ingredients except apricots and mulberries in a large bowl.

3. In a small sauce pan, gently heat coconut oil, tahini, honey/maple syrup, salt and vanilla powder until melted and well-combined. Pour over the dry mixture and combine until it's all coated.

4. Spread out the granola on a baking tray covered in parchment paper.

5. Toast in oven for about 20 minutes, or until golden and fragrant. Take it out once or twice during the baking time to stir, for a more even result. Don't worry if the granola still feels moist when you take it out. It will dry and crisp up once it cools.

6. Let cool completely before you add the apricot pieces and mulberries. Store in a large glass jar in the pantry. Lasts for about 2 weeks, if not longer.

Steel Cut Oatmeal with Mango, Berries, Nut Butter & Greek Yogurt

» Ingredients

· ¾ cup + 2 tablespoons steel cut oats
· 2 ½ cups water
· 1 teaspoon salt + extra
· 1 tablespoon coconut oil
· 1 teaspoon cinnamon
· ¼-½ cup almond milk

To serve
· Fresh mango
· Berries of choice
· Nut butter
· Greek yogurt
· Chopped nuts
· Almond milk
· Butter (optional)

Agnes: In Sweden, we traditionally serve this oatmeal only with a tablespoon of butter and sprinkled cinnamon on top. I like to pile mountains of toppings on mine though, so I typically raid the freezer and pantry for every nut, seed, berry and nut butter I can find. Adding a dollop of yogurt makes for an interesting, tangy contrast to the naturally sweet oats. Promise to try it!

The prepping of steel cut oats requires a little more planning than regular oatmeal, so I like to make a big batch at night that lasts me for 3 days.

» Method

1. The night before: Rinse steel cut oats thoroughly. Gently heat the coconut oil in a thick-bottomed sauce pan, then add oats and cinnamon. Cook on medium heat while stirring for approximately 2-3 minutes or until fragrant. Add water and salt and bring to boiling. Let simmer for about 3 minutes. Put the lid on the pan and turn the stove off. Let the pan rest on the stove until the morning.

2. In the morning: Gently heat the oatmeal with approximately ¼-½ cup almond milk and a pinch of salt. Start with a little almond milk and then add more if needed. Let simmer for a few minutes until desired consistency. Taste to see if the oats are done. They should be soft and chewy with a little bite. If they need to cook longer, add more milk. If you want to, you can stir in a tablespoon of butter.

3. Serve with fresh mango or other fruit, berries, chopped nuts, nut butter, a dollop of yogurt and a splash of almond milk. Enjoy!

Melissa Ofoedu

Blog/ **A Sweet Point of View**

"Ethiopian food, from traditional tomato stews to injera to classic Ethiopian coffee—the distinct smells and tastes evoke the most unique feelings of home, friendship and love to me."

A trained economist, Melissa Ofoedu runs the food blog "A Sweet Point of View" because of her passion for baking and food photography. She is especially interested in vegan baking and her recipes are a fusion of traditional African recipes and regional Austrian produce.

Ethiopian Coffee, the Smell of Homeland

Besides being well-known as the City of Music, Vienna is also famous for its fine pastries. Take for instance the *Apfelstrudel*—thin layers of flaky pastry enclosing tart cooking apples, sugar, cinnamon, raisins and breadcrumbs—a classic Viennese pastry that dates back to the Austro-Hungarian Empire.

Melissa Ofoedu was born and raised in this beautiful city of Vienna. Besides being an economist, she is also a recipe developer and photographer, sharing her creativity on her blog "A Sweet Point of View." Immersed in the culture of Vienna, Melissa has a passion for baking. But what makes her recipes unique is not only the Austrian influence, but also her African heritage.

"Eating and cooking have always been a family affair. It's where our family gathers, talks and enjoys food together," Melissa recalls. The food she ate at home was a mix of traditional Nigerian food and Austrian classics. From Nigerian plantains and yams to Austrian salty dumplings, these made up her diet growing up. During her childhood, she constantly participated in the cooking process with her siblings and parents.

In the recipes she created, she combines traditional African recipes and Austrian seasonal ingredients. One of the most sentimental recipes to her is Ethiopian Coffee Cakes with Styrian Apricot Ice Cream. It is created with the original Ethiopian coffee from the northern region of the country, which blends wonderfully with sweet-and-sour Styrian apricots, a perfect flavor explosion.

"The Ethiopian coffee is a component which strongly reminds me of my childhood," Melissa says. Coffee drinking was a big part of Sunday dinner parties. When coffee and cake were brought in, it meant the end of a successful gathering. The smell of Ethiopian coffee brings her back to those long weekends spent with a part of the family that was originally from Ethiopia. It has become an emblem that evokes the most unique feelings of home, friendship and love.

Those family memories made Melissa learn the importance of sharing food with the people she loves, and she appreciates the beauty of finding the time in a hectic and busy world to unwind, sit together and enjoy each other's company in the presence of delicious food.

1. *We learned that you were born and raised in Vienna, Austria. Could you let us know more about your upbringing in this beautiful city and how it has influenced your love for pastries?*

The French word for pastries is *Viennoiserie*, a word that solemnly describes what Vienna is known for around the world: fine pastry and baking. Growing up in Vienna, my love for baking was influenced by traditional Austrian and Viennese recipes. I grew up with the classic Sacher torte, apricot and poppy seed dumplings, and apple strudel, which is one of the first recipes I ever tried as a child. The seasonal ingredients in local markets, such as fresh strawberries from the lower Austrian valley, have influenced my creative recipes just as much as traditional ones.

2. *We know your recipes are deeply influenced by your heritage in Africa and its rich history. Which aspect of African food culture do you value, and how it is reflected in your recipes and cooking methods?*

Nigerian food often requires patience. The cooking process is uniquely time-consuming and inherently makes you value the food you eat. Slow food is probably just as much a part of Nigerian food culture as traditional herbs. What I value most about my West African heritage is that I discover new ingredients and recipes every day as I speak to my family and parents. In my recipes, I combine traditional recipes and seasonal local ingredients to create something new that my readers can relate to.

3. *What does your pantry look like?*

My pantry is pure chaos, from old cookbooks passed on from my mother and aunts, to a lot of raw ingredients like cocoa and coconut flour, to different oils, like almond oil, grape seed oils, and many more variations. I like to stock my pantry as well as possible and I have a large number of extras of each product in my pantry.

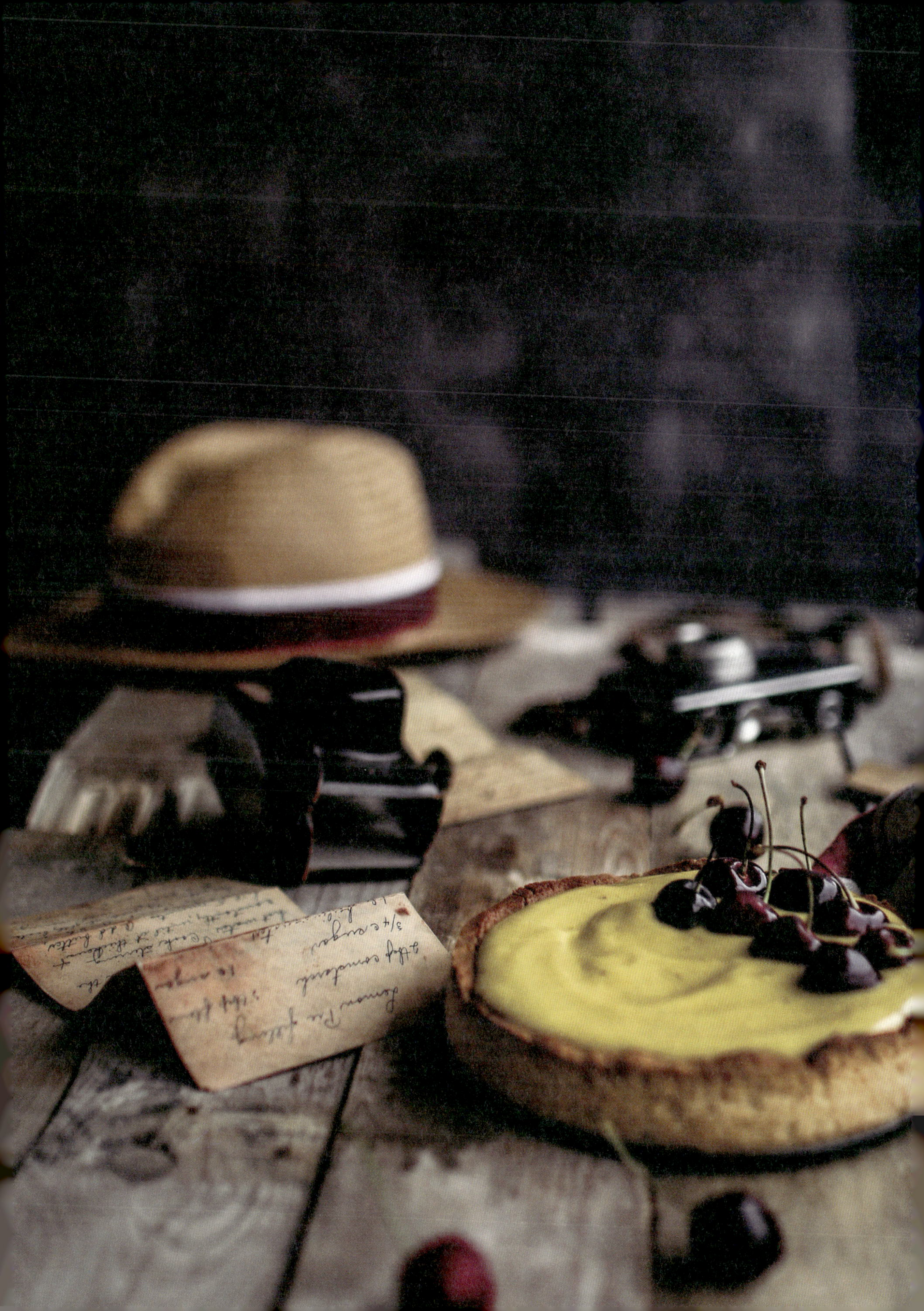

4. We know it's not easy to make vegan cake, so we assume that you must have been through a lot of processes to test the ingredients. What kind of obstacles and challenges have you met?

Surprisingly, the obstacles to making vegan cakes turned out to be not too challenging. Once you find the right ingredients to replace eggs, cream, etc., baking vegan becomes very easy. My go-to ingredients, to ensure that my pastries turn out just as good or even better than non-vegan versions, are vegan whipped cream, which tastes even better than dairy whipped cream, apple cider vinegar, sparkling water to ensure the fluffiness of a cake, and a lot of vegan butter or margarine. Whenever I bake vegan I am impressed by the properties of nature and the natural products that exist.

5. Besides food, you are also passionate about photography. How do you tell a story within a photo through food styling and light?

I always use natural light for my food photography. I believe natural light makes the food look the most natural and helps in achieving the styling and editing look that informs my food photography style. At the center of the stories in my pictures are the food, the ingredients and the history and tradition behind them. I use vintage props such as old scales and vintage cameras which I used as a child and inherited from my parents. Central to my photography is also making sure that the food looks natural and simple.

6. We know that you also love traveling and learning about other cultures. When you visit a foreign city, where do you like to go?

Whenever I travel, I immerse myself in the culture first. Depending on the country or city I am visiting, there are different things that I want to see. In Ghana, it might be the rich culture of food and sandy beaches; in Mexico, it would be the Aztec culture and Mayan ruins; and in Warsaw, the old Jewish quarter. The places I like to visit really always depend on the country or city, but the one thing crucial to any visit in any country is the food. The countries I love most are the ones that have a culture of serving street food. It is the easiest way to get to know local people and food.

Ethiopian Coffee Biscuit with Styrian Apricot Ice Cream

» Ingredients

Ethiopian coffee biscuit

- 2 cups (300 g) all-purpose flour
- ½ cup (120 g) coconut sugar
- 2 tablespoons ground Ethiopian Yirgacheffe
- 2 pinches of vanilla extract (or powder)
- 1 ¼ cups (300 ml) soda water
- ⅓ cup (70 ml) oil
- 1 tablespoon (16 g) powder
- 1 tablespoon of apple cider

Styrian apricot ice cream

- 1 cup (180 g) Xylitol sugar
- 1 pound (465 g) apricots
- 1 cup (250 ml) vegan whipped cream
- 2 teaspoons arrowroot flour

Styrian apricot compote

- ¼ cup (50 ml) water
- ½ cup (100 g) brown sugar
- ¼ pound (100 g) Styrian apricots
- ⅓ cup (80 g) vegan yogurt

» Method

1. To make Ethiopian coffee biscuits, mix all the dry ingredients. Then combine the liquid ingredients and slowly mix into the dry batter. Then fill 6 3" (6 cm) cake forms with the batter.

2. Bake the cakes for 35 minutes at 375ºF (190ºC). Let the cakes cool and cut off the top of the cakes to fill them with the cream and compote.

3. To make Styrian apricot ice cream, cool the vegan whipped cream in the refrigerator. (Cold whips up a lot faster.) Then whip the cream with the arrowroot flour for about 8 minutes or until stiff. Slowly add the sugar 1 spoon at a time.

4. Take out the pits from the apricots and cut the apricots into very small pieces. If they are very soft you can mash them. Then add the apricot pulp into the whipped cream. Then cool the ice cream for about 4 to 6 hours.

5. To make Styrian apricot compote, remove pits and place the apricots into a cooking pan. Add the water and cook the apricots until they are soft. Then add the sugar and let the apricots cook until dense.

6. Now add vegan yogurt and apricot compote onto the coffee cakes. Then top with the smaller part of the cake and the ice cream.

Lavender Poached Pears & Simple Crumble

» Ingredients

Lavender poached pears

· 3 pears

· 2 lavender stems

· ¾ cup (175 ml) water

Simple crumble

· ½ cup (100 g) birch sugar (or normal sugar)

· 1 cup (200 g) butter

· 2 ¼ cups (320 g) flour

» Method

1. To make lavender poached pears, put lavender stems into a pot with the peeled pears. Then cover pears with water and cook on low heat for about 25 minutes. The longer you cook the pears, the more intense the lavender flavor gets. Dry the pears and let them cool on plate.

2. To make the crumble, mix the birch sugar, butter and flour in a mixer and flatten out on a baking tray. Then bake for about 20 minutes or until light brown. Break the flat cake into crumbs and let them cool for 30 minutes. Then sprinkle crumble on pears.

Silvia Bifaro

Blog/ **Salvia+Limone**

"Those family Sundays shaped my love for daily celebration and cozy food as the way for celebrating slow living, love and family."

Silvia Bifaro is the creator behind the food blog "Salvia+Limone," where she shares vegan boutique cakes and other plant-based recipes. Originally from Italy, she now lives in London with her husband and two little children. She has a background as a fashion designer and a trained macrobiotic chef.

Love of Cozy Food

Silvia Bifaro is a happy mama of two lovely children. Besides taking care of her babies, her biggest passion is creating wholesome vegan cakes and decorating them like pieces of art. Through her careful selection of ingredients, Silvia proves that cake can be healthy and flavorful at the same time.

Her affection for healthy and delicious desserts has its roots in Liguria, the coastal region of northwestern Italy, which has a rich confectionery heritage. Growing up near Cinque Terre, Silvia is a child of that small piece of ocean and is tied to nature and traditional food. Since her childhood, healthy food has always been a big topic in her home. As former restaurant owners, her mom always cooked from scratch with local products and her dad made sure the food was beautifully presented. Every Sunday, there was a family gathering where traditional Ligurian dishes were served, and Silvia was an enthusiastic helper with food decoration and presentation. These moments are precious memories that still influence Silvia to this day.

She started cooking by herself when she found a macrobiotic shop in her town, which taught her how to make sushi, *onigiri* and *dashi* broth. She was so attracted by the aesthetic, the curated techniques and the possibilities of arranging the food on the plate like on a canvas. Although she had no idea what macrobiotic was,

it sowed a seed in her heart that blossomed ten years later.

The passion for food continued even when she was studying fashion design at university. She used food in conceptual art and behind the concept of her first catwalk. After graduation, she went on to work in the fashion industry. She was very immersed in her job, but the state of the fashion industry made her aware of humanity's high consumption of plastic and the stressful environment caused a eating disorder. Her beloved career came to cast a shadow on both her mental and physical health. Having decided to learn more, Silvia learned photography and joined the magazine *Marie Claire*. The talented photographers and stylists she assisted introduced her to macrobiotic food.

Things started to change when she moved to London. She pursued a professional culinary course and earned a degree as a macrobiotic chef, where she began her journey of self-nourishment. Macrobiotics is based on the Asian philosophy of *yin* and *yang*, encouraging people to seek balance in life for health and vitality. Through practices and self-healing, Silvia grew more aware of her humanity and her compassion towards herself and others.

Since then, macrobiotics has become the foundation of Silvia's cooking. Her family eats mostly a macrobiotic diet: unrefined grains, legumes, and a large variety of plant-based food. In the meantime, because she wanted something special for their celebrations that would remind her of those family Sundays, she started experimenting with making vegan cakes. She replaced the unhealthy ingredients with natural sugars, such as coconut sugar, dehydrated sugar or rice malt. Along with organic flours, the vegan cake would be more nutritious and more assimilable than the usual cakes. As a self-taught baker, Silvia says the most important thing is to be patient and organized during trial and error. When the cake is ready, Silvia always decorates it with beautiful flowers or other natural elements.

Nowadays, Silvia works as a food blogger, sharing recipes, styling tips and holding workshops through her blog "Salvia+Limone." On a normal day, she ends work at three o'clock in the afternoon to spend quality time with her children, either playing music or doing outdoor activities. When she is not away for workshops, she and her husband try to arrange at least one evening per week of undivided time as a couple. Although the well-planned schedule might seem intimidating to others, Silvia says it is her way to stay organized and make time to enjoy every aspect of her life.

1. When you moved to London, you attended a professional course and earned a degree as a macrobiotic chef. What did you learn during the courses?

Macrobiotics is a lifestyle born in western Europe against the developing fast-food culture, promoting a clean, sustainable diet of unrefined plant-based ingredients (brown rice, grains, legumes, seeds, vegetables and fruits) and avoiding any processed food. The diet involves very little food from animals, besides fish, and strictly no dairy. It takes the Eastern philosophy of *yin* and *yang* and applies it to food energies, and therefore its understanding goes beyond the nutritional value of food, and concentrates on the chakras, the emotions, the physical and sometimes the spiritual needs of the individual.

In short, the macrobiotic ideal plate includes all the chakra colors and all the five flavors, an array of leafy vegetables, roots, seeds or nuts, seaweeds, and a grain plus a legume. During the course, you learn to cook but also how to heal, support and nourish the body through food, shiatsu and other therapeutic techniques.

2. As a compassionate mother, the health of your kids must be one of your biggest concerns. Do you make special recipes for your kids?

My kids know plant-based natural food as a staple diet. We all eat the same food at the table—usually there is a large platter with many vegetables in the center, raw and cooked so each member can choose what they prefer. As special food, I make them tempura, finger food and sweet puddings, of course. They always have special cakes for their birthday parties and special treats for celebrations, so they never feel they are missing out. My kids' favorites vary from toasted *nori* to chia pudding or a Black Forest cake.

3. Your cakes look like pieces of art. What are your personal tips for decorating them?

Patience! Decor takes time so try not to rush it. Also try to work with the ingredients you have in your pantry or your garden before going to buy expensive flowers. Simple things enhance creativity more than the grand things. Place together a few of the decorations you have chosen and look how the colors and textures work together. Are they stimulating or flat? Are textures differentiated and interesting or are they too similar? Remember, less is more!

Let your imagination be as free as possible and enjoy the process—have fun! Try to have your ingredients at the right temperature—cool enough to be soft but firm, and the cake sponge a bit cool too. Always have free space in the fridge just in case your decor is taking too long and the cake starts to melt. You can quickly pop the whole thing in for a few minutes and then start again.

4. What is your view on the connection of diet and lifestyle? Does your culinary philosophy—consume less and use no animal products—also influence your lifestyle?

It does. When we decided to reduce animal products, we started with our lifestyle as well as with the diet. We listed all the products that we could cut or reduce significantly that were made using animals or that were not sustainable. From skincare products to clothes, plastic, paints, paper, magazines, etc.—literally everything, even plant food that is not fair. However, we did not throw away leather goods, plastic or clothes that we already had. Instead, we use them with even more respect and in general we aim to make all we buy last as long as possible.

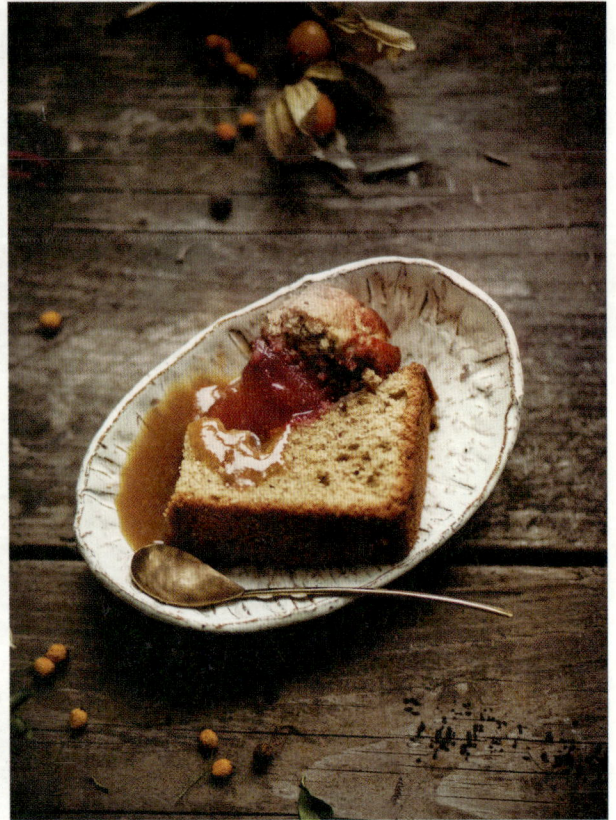

Pears and Cranberries Loaf Cake with Miso Salted Caramel

Utensils:

A medium loaf tin, small saucepan and a large bowl

» Ingredients

For the cake

- 1⅓ cups (200 g) white unbleached flour
- ⅔ cup (100 g) wholemeal flour (or use only 2 cups (300 g) white if you prefer)
- ⅓ cup (80 g) coconut sugar
- ½ teaspoon ground cardamom

- 2 tablespoons flax meal plus 6 tablespoons water
- ¾ cup (180 ml) extra virgin olive oil
- ½ cup (120 ml) water
- Dash of almond extract
- 2 to 3 medium pears, just ripe but not soft
- Cranberry pure juice, enough to roll the pears in (Silvia uses Abate Fetel pears).

For the oil-free caramel

- 4 tablespoons coconut or raw sugar of your choice
- 1 tablespoon plant milk at room temperature
- ½ tablespoon or more Hatcho Miso

» Method

1. Turn the oven on at 350°F (175°C). Grease the loaf tin with olive oil.

2. Wash and peel the pears. Then core them—with a small sharp knife, remove the bottom part and the seeds, creating a small narrow cone inside the fruits.

3. In a small saucepan, bring to heat the cranberry juice. Switch off and roll the pears in the juice until they are deep red (you can also use beet juice). Set aside.

4. Mix the 2 tablespoons of flax seeds with the 6 spoons of water in a small glass. Set aside for 5 minutes.

5. In a large bowl mix all the dry ingredients together.

6. In a jar also mix the liquid ingredients together.

7. Incorporate the flax seeds and the liquid ingredients in the dry and gently fold them together.

8. Pour the batter into the loaf tin. Immerse the 3 pears into the batter at equal distance.

9. Place the tin on the lowest rack of the oven and cook for 30 to 40 minutes depending on how much moisture your pears produce.

10. While the cake cooks, melt the 4 tablespoons of sugar in a small saucepan on a low flame. When it starts burning, gently add the milk. Be careful—it will splash—and whisk until combined. Turn off the heat and after a few minutes, incorporate the miso, tasting for quantity.

11. Enjoy this pear cake tepid or room temperature with a pour of the miso caramel sauce.

Pumpkin Coffee Cake with Mascarpone Amaretti Frosting and White Vanilla Chocolate

Utensils:

3 cake tins (5" or 12 cm),
springform or loose bottom.
A powerful food processor.
Mixing bowls.

» *Ingredients*

For the cake

· 2 cups flour (white or a mix with whole wheat)

· 1 ½ cups raw coconut or cane sugar (you can do half and half with Xylitol)

· ½ teaspoon of local unrefined salt

· 1 tablespoon baking powder

· 3 to 4 teaspoons coffee alternative or good quality ethical coffee (espresso or fine powder—no instant)

· 2 tablespoons flax meal + 8 teaspoons water

· ¼ cup extra virgin olive oil + 1 tablespoon for the pumpkin

· ⅓ cup plant-based yogurt

· ⅔ cup pureed pumpkin

· 2 teaspoons vanilla extract

· 1 cup water

» *Method*

To be made a day or two in advance

1. In a food processor pulse the sugar of your choice into an icing powder.

2. Again in a powerful food processor, make the cashews into a smooth cream, with the vanilla, coconut oil, the salt and the icing sugar you just made. Taste for sweetness. Let the cashew cream cool in the fridge for a few minutes.

3. Meanwhile, wash and cut half of a large pumpkin into small cubes. Roast the pumpkin with a pinch of salt and 1 tablespoon olive oil for 30 minutes at 400°F (200°C). Let them cool and pulse into a cream in a food processor. You will need ¾ cup of pumpkin cream. Store in the fridge.

4. In a mixing bowl, fold together the yogurt and the cooled cashew cream, adding the coffee powder. Taste for sweetness again.

5. Place in an airtight container and leave in the fridge overnight (at least) to set into a perfect consistency of a mascarpone cream. If you have any problem with consistency, gently pulse again with the addition of 1 tablespoon coconut oil and ½ teaspoon Xanthan gum, and leave to set again in the fridge for a couple of hours. However, if you drain the cashews well and the coconut yogurt is firm, you shouldn't have any problem at all.

The cake

1. Preheat the oven to 350°F (175°C). Grease the 3 cake tins (5" or 12 cm) with oil.

2. In a cup, soak the flaxseed powder with the 8 tablespoons water and leave to set for 5 minutes.
In a large bowl mix all the dry ingredients. And in a large jar mix all the wet ingredients, adding the soaked flaxseeds. Combine the wet to the dry ingredients in the bowl, gently folding them together. Be sure all is well-combined before pouring in the cake tins.

For the mascarpone filling and frosting (to be prepared the day before)

· 2 cups (300 g) soaked overnight and well-drained cashews
· 1 ¼ cups (300 g) very firm coconut yogurt
· 1 tablespoon coconut oil
· 7 to 10 teaspoons Xylitol or raw icing sugar (or to taste)
· 2 teaspoons vanilla extract
· 1 teaspoon coffee powder, same as in the cake
· ½ teaspoon salt
· 10 to 13 vegan amaretti biscuits* (optional, can be replaced with very crunchy and light biscuits). Keep the best 7 for the topping decor.

* amaretti are a very light kind of biscuit (caloric, yes, but not dense) made of bittersweet almonds and egg whites. There are 2 kinds: soft and hard. In this cake you need the hard type. You can find the vegan version at healthy shops and online. If you need to replace amaretti use very crunchy cookies that will not soak up the filling.

For the dripping chocolate

· ¾ cup (130 g) good-quality vegan white chocolate
· 1 tablespoon vanilla extract

3. Pour the batter in the tins equally. Cook for 45 to 50 minutes, or until the toothpick comes out clean.

4. Let the cakes cool in the tins until they are tepid, remove from the tins and let them finish to cool in the fridge.

5. Meanwhile, on a low flame, in a bain-marie, melt the white chocolate with the vanilla extract. The water should never start boiling. Leave to cool down until slightly tepid but still runny enough to be poured—a honey-like consistency.

Assembling and decor

1. If the cakes are too rounded on top, cut them straight with a long bread knife.

2. Place the first cake on a desired plate and scoop abundant mascarpone to make ½" (1 cm)-thick filling, sprinkle with broken amaretti and push them down gently in the filling. Cover with the second cake and repeat. Now place the third cake on top, but upside down, so the perfect bottom becomes the top of your layered cake. Scoop abundant frosting on top and with a spatula, start distributing it to the edges and down the side. Fill up any holes and gently scrape away any extra. If the frosting becomes runny, move it and the cake into the fridge for 30 minutes.

3. Silvia likes her cakes to have a naked frosting, as they feel lighter than fully covered cakes, but you are welcome to cover it fully if you prefer.

4. Once finished with the frosting, pour on top ¾ of your white chocolate. As it starts to drip nicely, move the cake straight back to the fridge.

5. Mix the leftover chocolate with some frosting (no need to measure, ¼ cup frosting is roughly what you will have left) and fill a piping bag prepared with a star pipe.
Place the piping bag in the fridge as well for a few minutes.

6. When stiff enough, pipe 7 biscuits with this mixture, and dust with coffee powder. Distribute the biscuits on the top along the edge of the cake.

7. Chill before cutting. Enjoy!

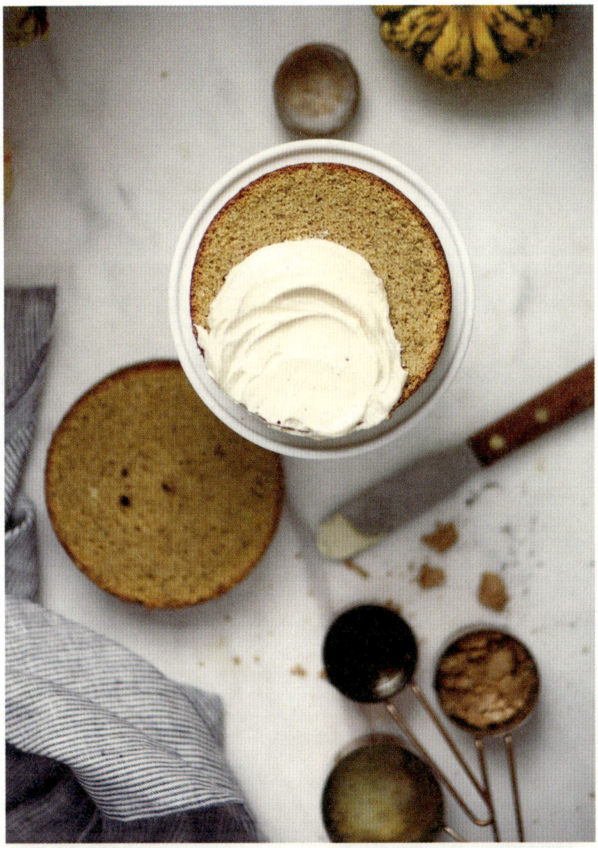
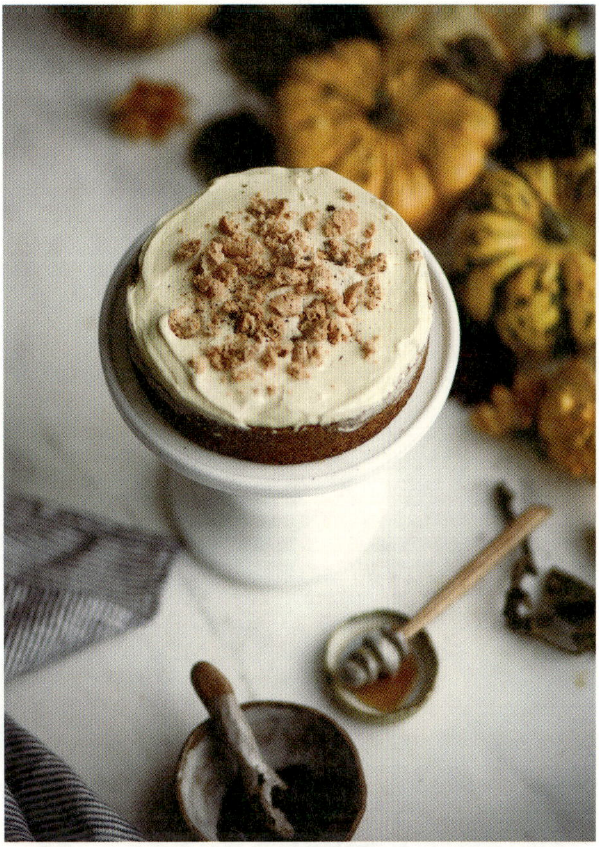
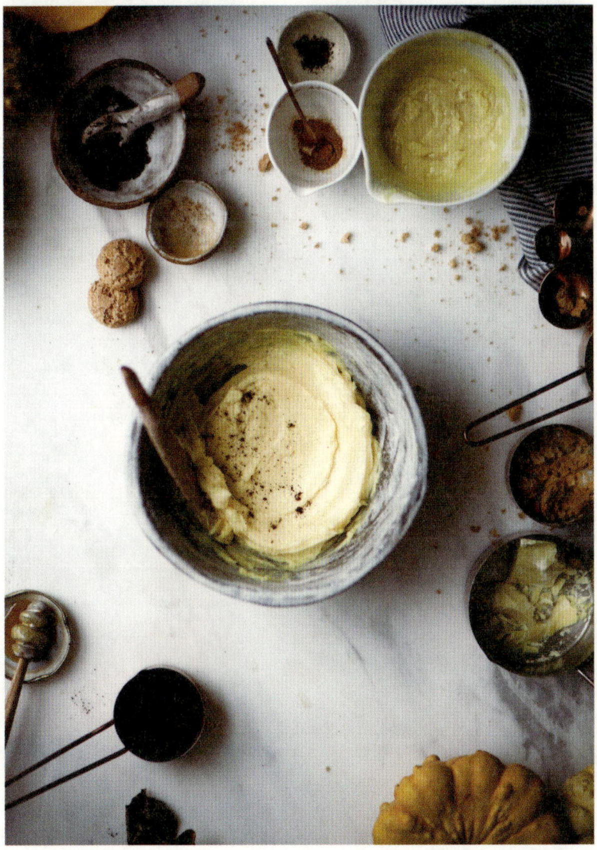
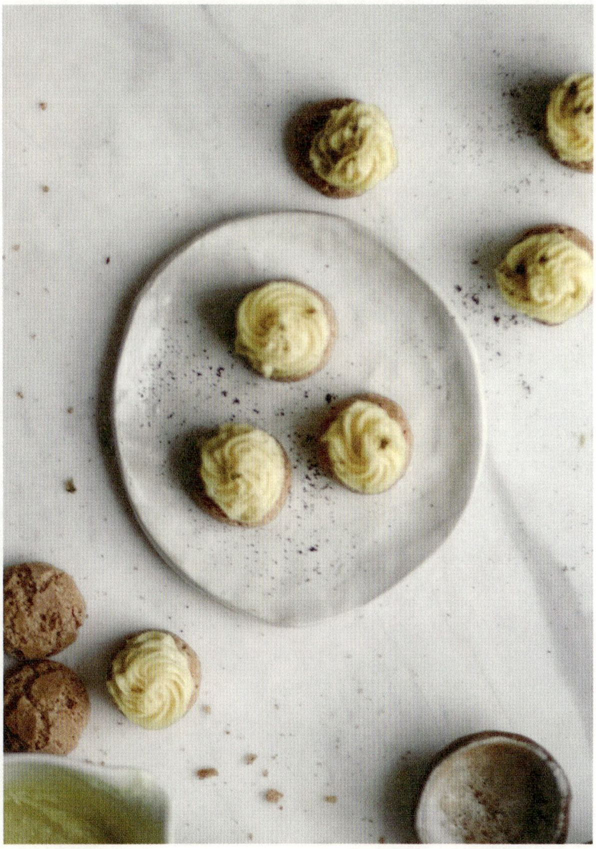

Meg van der Kruik

"I choose to embrace the mess as best as I can. It isn't always pretty, but at the end of the day, as long as we are all healthy, happy, and well-fed, my primary job is done."

Meg van der Kruik lives in Atlanta, Georgia, with her husband, two kids and a lovely dog. Although the family has different types of eating habits and tolerances, Meg manages to bring them together around their family table every night.

This Mess Is Ours

Meg van der Kruik is one of those people with a big family for whom things usually get pretty messy at dinner times, but she has her own secret for bringing everyone around and making them satisfied.

Meg fell in love with cooking at an early age. She created, styled, and photographed the dishes in a fictitious cookbook she was writing when she was eight years old. As the daughter of a pastry chef, her very first job was helping her mom in the family bakery and scooping ice cream cones at their local ice cream shop. Throughout her career, she kept herself busy in the food industry, running coffee shops, waiting tables, and working in kitchens—cooking has always been the comfort and cure when she was bored.

A few years ago, after her infant son was diagnosed with a gluten allergy, she dedicated herself to learning to make meals the whole family would love. Her family is the representation of a modern family, with many different dietary preferences: her husband is vegetarian, while the two kids are meat lovers; her husband and son have gluten intolerances, but her teenage girl is very picky about gluten-free food.

Since then, Meg has experimented with a lot of recipes that try to cater to everyone's needs. The family eats mostly vegetarian, while meat dishes are served only a few times a week. If they are having a vegetarian meal, Meg comforts her meat-loving son with other food he likes, such as a variety of fruit as a side, or a peanut butter-and-jam sandwich. She has also developed a blend of gluten-free flours that turns out so tender and fluffy that meets her daughter's testing standards.

Although everyone has different preferences, the family has a handful of staple dishes that everyone likes. A big bowl of pasta smothered in homemade pasta sauce, burrito bowls, and fried rice are always a win every time they make their way to the table. With her success in attracting everyone around the dinner table, Meg hopes to help more families answer the frustrating question: What's for dinner? The more than 500 recipes documented on her blog "This Mess is Ours" provide useful guidance for families with special dietary needs.

Meg's obsession with food also has an influence on her family members. Her teenage daughter, Eliza, is a delightful partner during cooking sessions, and aspires to work in a bakery after high school. Her husband, Todd, who is Vice President of Global Design for a flooring manufacturer, doubles as a food stylist and photographer, and the most willing recipe tester during weekends. There is no argument that food has tightened the bonds between family members.

Leaving their sweet home in Long Beach, California, the family relocated across the country in the summer of 2018 to settle in Atlanta, in southeastern America. They are all very excited about their upcoming adventures and cannot wait to immerse themselves in Southern food and culture.

1. You named your blog "This Mess is Ours." What are some occasions when you are happy with the "mess," and are there any occasions you become frustrated?

Well, mostly I try to embrace the mess. However, I do sometimes like everything to have a moment where it feels perfect, like holiday dinner! With kids and a very active family, that is almost an impossible task. It never fails—I get amped up about everything being in the perfect place and looking a certain way before our guests arrive. But once everyone is here, I quickly realize that it is the people who feast with us that bring the magic to the moment. While we will all definitely remember the good times we had visiting with one another, sharing a meal, no one is going to remember if the shelves were a little cluttered, there were toys on the floor, or the flowers didn't turn out exactly as anticipated.

2. We know it's not easy to prepare meals that take care of the dietary restrictions of each family member and make everyone happy. What kind of experiments or learning processes have you gone through to satisfy everyone at the dinner table?

I have had a lot of success at our dinner table in creating meals that all four of us love, but that is only because I have had at least three times as many failures! My crew can be pretty picky at times, so I try not to get too frustrated if something doesn't get as many "oohs" and "ahhs" as I wanted it to. Sometimes, all it takes is a few simple tweaks to the ingredients, so the next time I make it I can win my crew over, but some recipe ideas are just duds and that is okay, too.

3. What's your tip for keeping everyone happy and focused at the family dinner table?

I try to offer something for everyone, every night. For me it is really important that we all gather once a day at the family table to reconnect and spend time with one another. We like to include fun activities at the dinner table like card and board games. No matter what we are serving to eat, our kids know we are always serving a good time, so they are happy to ditch their devices and make their way to the dinner table every night.

4. Could you share one occasion when your food or preparation made a marvelous impression on your family and your friends?

I think anytime you create a meal for someone from your heart, it really shows and makes an impression, so it's hard to pinpoint just one. However, when we have friends or family over for a big feast, I like to sometimes serve up a homemade falafel feast with all of the trimmings. Everyone always gets so excited when the food starts rolling out of the kitchen—herbaceous falafel, homemade tzatziki, freshly made naan bread—it's pure dinnertime magic!

5. What is your culinary philosophy?

I don't know that I have a culinary philosophy per se, but food is the one thing that I refuse to argue about with my family. My husband has been a vegetarian for most of his life, but we didn't enforce that on our children. Instead we offer them lots of great vegetarian options to try and to make their own opinions about, but we also serve them the meat-based dishes that they really like as well.

There are so many things in this world worthy of causing a ruckus over, but I just never want food to be a place of stress or tension for my family. I feel like the family table should be a safe zone for all of us to gather and share what has happened in our daily lives. As long as I am offering healthy choices at our dinner table, I figure it doesn't really matter what they choose to eat a serving of. Of course, I would love it if my seven-year old son ate my newest cauliflower creation, but you know what? He may just not be ready and that is okay. I praise him if he tries new things, while I make sure he is doubling up on things I'm serving each night that I know he really loves.

Broccoli and Ricotta Lasagna Rolls

» Ingredients

· 1 can (28 ounces) petite diced tomatoes

· 1 small red onion, halved and peeled

· 5 tablespoons unsalted butter

· Kosher salt and pepper to taste

· 2 eggs

· 1 pound ricotta cheese

· 12 ounces part-skim mozzarella cheese, shredded and divided

· 2 ounces Parmigiano-Reggiano cheese, finely grated

· 1 crown of broccoli, cut into florets and steamed

· 12 gluten-free lasagna noodles, cooked until *al dente*

» Method

1. Preheat the oven to 350°F (175°C).

2. Combine the tomatoes, red onion halves and butter in a saucepan over medium-high heat. Season with salt and pepper then bring to a boil. Reduce to a simmer and cook, stirring occasionally for 15 minutes. Remove from the heat, discard the onion halves and set the sauce aside.

3. Combine the eggs, ricotta, ½ of the shredded mozzarella, and the Parmigiano-Reggiano cheese. Season with salt and pepper and stir to combine.

4. In the bowl of a food processor fitted with the "S" blade pulse the steamed broccoli until it is broken down into small uniform pieces. Add the riced broccoli to the ricotta mixture and stir to combine.

5. Spread ½ cup of the pasta sauce in an even layer across the bottom of a 13" x 9" baking pan. Then, working with one lasagna noodle at a time, blot any liquid off the noodle and then spread ⅓ cup of the ricotta mixture onto the top of the noodle, then carefully roll the noodle from end to end, beginning at a short side. Place the rolled lasagna noodles seam-side down into the baking dish. Repeat the process with the remaining pasta and ricotta mixture until the baking pan is full.

6. Spread the remaining sauce over the top of the lasagna rolls and sprinkle with the remaining shredded mozzarella cheese.

7. Bake in the oven for 20 minutes until the cheese is melted and the sauce is bubbling. Serve immediately.

Vegan Sheet Pan Shawarma

» Ingredients

· Juice of 2 lemons

· ½ cup olive oil

· 6 cloves garlic, smashed and minced

· 1 teaspoon kosher salt

· 2 teaspoons freshly ground black pepper

· 2 teaspoons ground cumin

· 1 teaspoon coriander

· 2 teaspoons sweet paprika

· 1 teaspoon turmeric

· 1 teaspoon Aleppo pepper flakes

· ½ teaspoon ground cinnamon

· 1 large head of cauliflower broken into small florets

· 1 can of chickpeas, drained and rinsed

· 2 small red onions, quartered

· 1 (8-ounce package) gluten-free tempeh cut into cubes

· 1 whole lemon, halved for roasting on pan

· Optional garnishes: cilantro or micro green cilantro, sliced green onions.

Notes:

· If you don't have a sheet pan that is as large as in the photograph, you can use 2 smaller sheet pans and divide the ingredients between them.

· If you are not a fan of tempeh, you can replace it with firm tofu.

» Method

1. Preheat oven to 400°F (200°C) and line a 13" x 18" baking sheet with parchment paper.

2. In a large mixing bowl, combine the lemon juice, olive oil, garlic, salt, pepper, cumin, coriander, paprika, turmeric, Aleppo pepper flakes, and cinnamon. Whisk to combine. Divide the marinade into 2 bowls.

3. Add the tempeh to the first bowl, turning to coat each piece in the marinade. Set aside for 10 minutes to marinate.

4. Add the cauliflower florets and chickpeas to the second bowl, turning the ingredients together with a large spoon or tongs until all of the vegetables are coated.

5. Arrange the tempeh on the sheet pan first, spooning any remaining marinade from the bowl on top of the pieces. Next, add the seasoned cauliflower and chickpeas to the pan around the tempeh. Layer in the onion quarters and place the 2 lemon halves, cut side down on the pan, one near the top and one near the bottom.

6. Bake for 25 to 30 minutes or until the tempeh is warmed through and the vegetables are tender.

7. To serve, squeeze the roasted lemon halves over the tempeh and vegetables and then garnish with desired toppings. Serve immediately.

Lydia Wong

Blog/ **Ginger and Chorizo**

"Growing up in a big family, we were lucky to have Mother cooking for us every single day and it really made an impact on our later lives, and led us to appreciate home-cooked food as much as spending time with our loved ones."

Lydia Wong is the writer and recipe developer behind the food blog "Ginger and Chorizo." Having grown up in Macau, and having spent almost two decades in Europe, her cooking style is influenced by both Chinese and Western cuisine.

Cooking as a Way of Passing down the Tradition

Lydia Wong is a happy mama living in Berlin with her husband and her nine-year-old daughter. Apart from being a food stylist and writing about food, looking after her family and cooking nourishing food for them are among her most enjoyable things to do.

Lydia was born and raised in Macau. As a teenager, she often had to help her mom prepare food for their big family and it was then when her passion for food started. Her mom was a great cook and Lydia learned a lot of cooking skills from her, such as understanding the characteristics of the ingredients, flavor pairing, being creative with food combinations, and being patient and managing her time well. Most importantly, though, she learned to taste the food as she is cooking it, and to adjust the seasonings accordingly. The valuable advice helped her master the basics of home cooking. "My mother always told us that it is very important to love food, to enjoy cooking for yourself and others. Every dish will taste wonderful if you cook it with some love," Lydia says.

Apart from her mother's home cooking, the colonized Portuguese cuisine, Macanese, was also an important influence on her cooking. She recalls dining in restaurants with her father, eating grilled chorizo and poached *bacalhau* (dried and salted cod). The special flavors of Macanese food left her a lasting memory,

motivating her to try pairing Portuguese and Chinese ingredients and methods in her own cooking.

In her early twenties, Lydia moved to London to pursue an interior design degree. After graduation, she worked as a personal assistant to a restaurateur who was expanding his business at the time. Lydia's main responsibilities were to help the owner run the restaurants, contribute design ideas to the new restaurants, manage the design projects, branding and marketing. During that six years of working in the food industry, Lydia obtained valuable experience such as meeting many great cooks and tasting many delicious foods, as well as learning more about the industry's operational and social aspects.

After Lydia and her family relocated to Berlin in 2009, she became a stay-at-home mom which made it possible for her to get into cooking for her family again. Most of the time, she cooks Chinese food, European food, or a fusion in between; on other occasions, she experiments with new recipes and she finds that she is very lucky to have a husband and a daughter who are very open to new tastes.

The city of Berlin provides rich soil for her to be creative with food. She began her food blog "Ginger and Chorizo" in 2014, and also works as a food stylist,

having done props and food styling work for a well-known Japanese food company called Ajinomoto.

"When I first moved to Berlin nearly nine years ago, the food scene is Berlin was still relatively mundane," Lydia says. "But during the recent years, Berlin has become a cosmopolitan city and international cuisines are popping up all over the city. People are also very open to new ideas." Lydia recalled that she once did an *onigiri* event, during which she not only satisfied her urge to cook for people around the world, but also built up many connections with creative people.

Almost two decades away from her homeland, Lydia sometimes misses the familiar flavors that she grew up with, which is why she determined to re-create the flavors she once adored by cooking and recording her food journey on her blog. While the cooking skills acquired in Macau are the fundamentals, the diverse food scenes in Europe have opened up her eyes to endless possibilities of working with food, encouraging her to be more creative and experimental.

1. What was the first dish that you learned to cook?

I can't really remember precisely since I have learned a lot of dishes from my mother throughout the years. But the most vivid one is her special spicy fermented black bean sauce, which is featured in my ramen recipe (page 171). I remember how she mashed the black beans with the end of the knife handle together with crushed garlic, and how she stirred the sauce to combine all the rest of the ingredients. She usually cooked the sauce with sliced beef filets and lots of crunchy vegetables, and the aroma would fill up the whole kitchen. We would then gobble it down with steamy hot rice.

2. Could you give us an example of a dish that exemplifies the way Macanese cuisine lies in between Portuguese and Chinese cooking?

Macau Fried Rice (recipe featured on page 168) is a very good example of what Macanese food is all about: the unique combination of ingredients and cooking techniques of the East and West. Fried rice is one of the most popular dishes in Chinese cuisine, whereas chorizo and olive are two of the most important ingredients in the Portuguese kitchen. Furthermore, one of the staple rice dishes in Portugal is "tomato rice," which explains the tomato paste we use in this recipe. The whole dish is seasoned with soy sauce instead of salt, which again is a mixture of flavor from the East and West. I added my own twist to this recipe, as edamame is not a usual ingredient in Macau Fried Rice.

3. Can you share an interesting story from your days working in the London restaurant?

I admired all the cooks I met during those years because they were all hard-working and genuine people. I was lucky to be able to enjoy the food they cooked regularly and it is something I am still grateful for. I remember during one of the peak lunch hours, I was working behind the reception (where my office was) and realized that all the customers wanted to have sushi, but we only had one sushi chef on duty that day. So I was very brave to step behind the sushi counter, where I rolled up my sleeves and started making sushi alongside our chef. It was really fun and I remember how impressed the chef was when we managed to settle all orders without one single complaint! I was very proud of myself for a long time!

4. What is your culinary philosophy now?

Be a responsible consumer, whether you are the one who cooks or the one who eats. Be creative and don't be afraid of trying out new food. As always, cook with love and to use food and eating to connect with people.

5. I read on your Instagram feed that your first fictional short story, "Naila," was just published in a magazine. Would you like to share a few words about your love of writing?

Yes! I love to write, and always have since I was a little girl. I am a typical introvert and I found I could express myself better through writing. Sometimes I write to make sense of something which is otherwise a little difficult to comprehend. Sometimes I write in order to dive into a completely different world.

Macau Fried Rice

Serves 4

» Ingredients

· 1 cup (250 g) uncooked long grain rice, washed and drained (or 4 portions of leftover cooked rice)

· 1⅔ cups (400 ml) chicken or vegetable stock (or water)

· ½ tablespoon of olive oil

· 1 heaping tablespoon tomato puree

· 3 tablespoons soy sauce

· A small pinch of sugar

· 1 teaspoon of sesame oil (optional)

· ½ cup (100 g) chorizo, diced

· 1 small onion, finely chopped

· ⅔ cup (100 g) frozen edamame or green peas

· ⅔ cup (80 g) black olives, halved

» Method

1. Warm olive oil in a medium saucepan, add rice and fry for a minute, then carefully pour in the stock (or water) and mix well with the rice, bring it to boil.

2. Cover and turn down to a low simmer until all the liquid is absorbed—around 7 to 10 minutes. Check if the liquid is all gone then remove from heat and place a clean kitchen towel on the saucepan and cover it with the lid, and let it stand for another 5 minutes. The towel will absorb the steam and condensation from the hot rice, keeping the rice light and fluffy. After the 5 minutes, fluff the rice up with a fork or spatula.

3. Transfer the rice onto a large baking tray (or platter) lined with baking paper. Spread it out as much as possible—it allows the rice to cool down quickly and prevents it from sticking, which makes frying easier!

If you are using leftover rice, start from the step below.

4. In a small bowl, combine tomato puree, soy sauce, sugar and sesame oil, mix well and set aside.

5. Heat a large, deep, non-stick pan (a wok is ideal) on high, drizzle a little olive oil, add the chorizo and stir fry until the chorizo turns slightly brown (be careful not to burn it) and releases its paprika oil. With a slotted spoon, transfer the chorizo into a bowl and set aside, leaving the paprika oil in the pan.

6. Add the onion and a small pinch of salt to the pan, fry on medium heat until the onion starts to soften, about 1 to 2 minutes. Add the rice and turn the heat to high, break up any lumps and continue to stir fry for a further 2 to 3 minutes.

7. Drizzle over the soy sauce and tomato puree mixture, fry and make sure everything is coated with the sauce. Add edamame and stir fry for another 2 minutes or until the beans are warm through. Now add the chorizo and stir fry again until all is combined. Have a taste and adjust the seasoning if needed. Remove from the heat. Finally, add the olives and mix well. Serve warm or at room temperature.

Braised Spicy Aubergine Ramen

Serves 2

» Ingredients

· 1 medium aubergine (eggplant), cut into bite-sized pieces (or ½ of a large one)

· 2 large mushrooms (4 ounces, 120 g), brushed clean, cut into bite-sized pieces

· ½ red bell pepper, deseeded and cut into bite-sized pieces

· ½ small carrot, sliced into coins

· 1 small onion, roughly chopped

· A large handful of broccoli florets (or stems), roughly chopped

· Vegetable oil

· 1 ¼ cups (300 ml) water, plus more

· 2 cakes ramen

· 1 chili, finely chopped (for garnish)

· A few sprigs of fresh parsley, leaves picked and roughly chopped (for garnish)

For the sauce

· 1 tablespoon fermented black bean (you can find it in the Asian store)

· 1 clove of garlic, minced

· 1 tablespoon tamari (or soy sauce)

· 1 tablespoon oyster sauce

· 1 teaspoon miri

· 2 teaspoons Shaoxing rice wine (or sake)

· 1 teaspoon sesame oil

· 1 heaping teaspoon *sambal oelek* (plus more if you prefer spicier)

· Small pinch of coconut sugar (or honey)

» Method

1. Cook ramen according to package instructions. Drain and drizzle sesame oil and mix well to prevent sticking. Set aside.

2. Put the black bean into a small bowl and mash with the end of your knife or the end of a rolling pin, add minced garlic and the rest of the sauce ingredients, mix well and set aside.

3. Warm 2 tablespoons of vegetable oil in a nonstick pan or wok, add aubergine and brown on all sides, cook until aubergine is slightly soft and translucent. Transfer them to a plate lined with kitchen paper to absorb excess oil. Set aside.

4. In the same pan, heat 1 tablespoon of oil until hot. Add onion, carrot, broccoli, bell pepper, mushroom and stir fry for a couple of minutes, add a splash of water and carry on stirring for another minute. Add the spicy black bean sauce in the mix and 1 ¼ cups (300 ml) of water to the pan. Bring to boil and add the aubergine.

5. Turn the heat down and let it simmer for about 2 minutes. Push the vegetables to one side of the pan and add the ramen to the sauce, stir until the ramen is coated evenly with the sauce.

6. Divide and transfer the ramen into 2 warm bowls and then spoon the remaining vegetables over the ramen. Garnish with chopped chili and chopped parsley. Serve immediately.

Kathrin Salzwedel

Blog / **Klara's Life**

"We want to show other people how easy cooking is and they can also have a lot of fun doing this together with their families or by themselves."

Kathrin Salzwedel is the creator behind the food and lifestyle blog "Klara's Life." Based in a small town in Germany, her cooking style is influenced by nature, colors and emotions. Through her simple, homestyle recipes, she wishes to encourage others to have fun in the kitchen.

Have Fun Creating
a Simple Dish

The reason that many people are enthralled by home cooking is not only creating flavors, but also the ability to mix different textures and color combinations, treating each dish as a work of art. Kathrin Salzwedel is one of these people. Looking at her food photos, it is hard not to call her a color master in home cooking.

Kathrin lives in a small town in the southwest of Germany called Herrenberg, which is close to the Black Forest nature reserve and the Swabian Alps. Having grown up near mountains and lakes, Kathrin has an intrinsic love for nature: she had a horse while growing up, and now she has a dog and a cat, and she also raises seven chickens in the garden. It is a pleasure for her to watch the chickens running around in the area. The organic eggs provided by those chickens are also an important ingredient in Kathrin's homemade dishes.

In 2016, Kathrin started her blog "Klara's Life," and in July 2017, her boyfriend Ramin came on board. Together, the couple creates simple homestyle dishes, mostly plant-based or with their organic eggs. Sometimes they make typical German food, like stews and soups; other times they test new flavors, mixing Asian food with Western styles like coconut milk with Brussels sprouts. Throughout the years, Kathrin says her cooking style has been influenced a lot by Ramin, who is also a great cook. "Because my boyfriend has a combined heritage from Germany and Iran, I have learned to cook Persian food from him," Kathrin says. She also describes Ramin's cooking as "freestyle," which encourages her to have an open mind towards cooking. For example, she will pick out five ingredients, looking at the color and texture and figuring out the herbs that will make them work together. "The best cooking skill is trying! If you make mistakes, you know how you can make it better at the next time."

Besides learning from her boyfriend and traditional German cooking, Kathrin is also a big fan of culinary books. She has read about the ayurvedic kitchen, the raw kitchen, and cooking in other continents and nations. "You are asking yourself, 'Can I use this information for my own work?' And yes, it influences your way of cooking in a fascinating and rich way."

Cooking has become an essential and inseparable part of her life. Home cooking not only guarantees the safety and health of the dish, but also allows people to be creative in the kitchen. Talking about her future plans, Kathrin says she wishes to write a cookbook and hold cooking workshops with her boyfriend.

1. What is your culinary philosophy?

I'm trying to use fresh and local products. I like to go to the market and support local distributers. Mixing different kinds of cooking styles and picking out some tricks from influencers, such as my boyfriend or the traditional cooking in my home country, are useful. And I always want to have fun in the kitchen, which means that music becomes a part of cooking, or having conversation or watching people passing by.

2. Among all the recipes you have created, which one is the most memorable or has special meaning to you?

I really like pasta. It is easy to cook and there are so many ways to cook it! You can serve it cold and warm, with raw vegetables, with hot sauces in many different colors, and many different ways. They can be served as salads, gratins, starters, mains or desserts.

And I love my grandma's hazelnut cake. It's the best and takes me back to my childhood. It was also my birthday cake every year.

3. Has the experience of learning fashion design influenced your food styling? In what ways?

I love fashion and I was always fascinated by design and beautiful things. Esthetic, handcrafted work is the basis of both cooking and fashion. Good design is in one way the result of knowledge, experience, esthetics, courage and a good technique. These skills are a lifelong learning process, not only in professional training in universities but also daily life. I don't want to merely shoot food; I also want to tell stories with my pictures and motivate people to be creative in life.

4. Besides cooking healthy food, what other things are you interested in?

I love interior design, traveling, fashion, calligraphy, nature and animals. I love to create my living environment, so I paint my walls in different colors and in different ways. I love accessories. The arrangement of different parts and the composition of details are very interesting.

Raspberry Pull-Apart Bread with Cinnamon Dust

» Ingredients

· 1 ¼ cups (300 ml) milk, lukewarm (optional oat milk)
· 5 tablespoons (90 g) soft vegan butter
· 2 ½ cups (475 g) flour (type 550)
· ½ cube fresh yeast
· ¼ cup (50 g) of sugar
· 1 organic egg
· Raspberry jam or jam of your choice
· 1 tablespoon of vegan butter
· Cinnamon sugar mixture

» Method

1. Pour the flour into a mixing bowl, make a trough, add the yeast into the crumbs and add about ¼ cup (50 ml) of warm milk plus a pinch of sugar, mix briefly and cover with flour. Leave for 5 to 10 minutes. Add egg, sugar, the remaining lukewarm milk and soft butter. Knead the dough for several minutes to form a smooth soft dough. The dough should not be too sticky.

2. Cover with a kitchen towel and leave it in a warm place for about 1 hour until the dough has doubled.

3. Roll on a well-floured baking paper. Cut into 5 strips. Sprinkle with 2 tablespoons of raspberry jam or jam of your choice.

4. Overlay the strips. Cut into 5 to 6 square-shaped rectangles.

5. Place them in a baking tray with baking paper. Let it rest for a minute.

6. Heat the oven to 350ºF (175ºC). Sprinkle the cake with butter flakes, cinnamon and sugar mixture.

7. Bake on the middle rack for 25 minutes. If it gets too dark, cover with baking paper.

8. Leave to cool for 20 to 30 minutes.

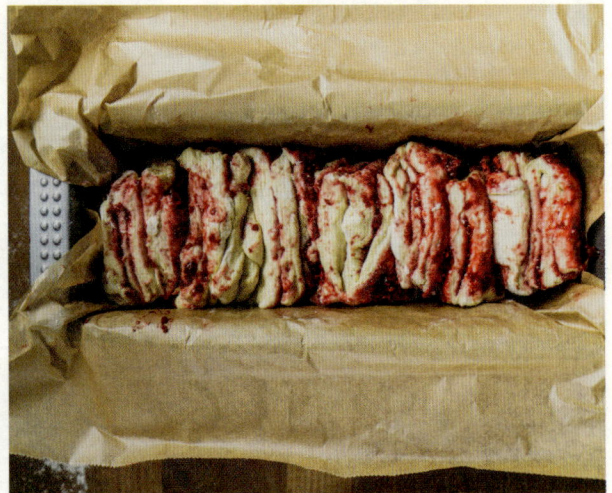

Spicy Cardamom Cranberry Cubes

» Ingredients

· ½ cup (100 g) of coconut sugar
· 1 cup (200 g) vegan butter, soft
· 1 teaspoon vanilla paste
· 2 organic eggs
· ¾ cup (100 g) spelt flour
· 1 teaspoon cinnamon
· 1 teaspoon cardamom
· ⅓ cup (40 g) cranberries, chopped
· ¼ cup (20 g) almonds, chopped
· Salt

» Method

1. Pre-heat the oven to 350°F (175°C).

2. Beat the butter, sugar, eggs, vanilla and spices creamy with the whisk of a hand mixer or the food processor.

3. Stir in the flour.

4. Spread the dough in a square baking pan (9" or 23 cm) lined with baking paper.

5. Sprinkle with cranberries and almonds and bake for 20 to 30 minutes. Make a stick sample. If the cake is too dark, cover with aluminum foil.

6. Allow to cool and cut.

7. Stored in a tin box, the cubes last about 2 weeks.

Viola Hou

IG/ **Thesunshineeatery**

"It's important to keep a good balance between healthy eating and treating yourself because it's that balance that keeps us sane and happy."

Viola Hou is a German foodie who runs "The Sunshine Eatery," which is both an Instagram account and a YouTube channel. She loves healthy eating and Asian cuisines.

Balanced Eating:
the Secret to Energetic Life

As a Master's student in business psychology, cooking is the biggest outlet for Viola Hou to unleash creativity. On her Instagram account "The Sunshine Eatery" she shares her daily food, from Vietnamese summer rolls to vegetarian burgers. The positive vibe in her photos echoes the old saying: You are what you eat.

Viola was born and raised in Germany. As a family of ethnic Chinese, the food they prepared at home was typical Chinese food centered on steamed rice, stir-fried dishes and soup. One of her favorite foods is her parents' homemade chive dumplings. They grow their own chives in the garden, and Viola has been helping to fold the dumplings since she was a little girl, so dumplings always hold a special place in her heart and remind her of home.

Her interest in food grew tremendously in high school, when she discovered many food blogs and saved recipes she wanted to re-create. When she researched more about food, her perspective towards what she ate also changed. Previously, she just happily enjoyed food that tasted good, but now she takes a second thought, and prefers things that are good for her body.

It was during her later college years when she started experimenting more with healthy eating. She has been mostly vegan for over three years now, but her emphasis was never on a particular way to eat or labeling herself a certain way. What she really wants is to cook food that is nutrient-dense and healthy. That's why her recipes use lots of vegetables, whole grains, beans and legumes, fruit and natural sweeteners such as maple syrup or dates.

Once in a while, Viola treats herself to a nice dinner out with friends and enjoys a glass of wine. She has dark chocolate almost every day after dinner and has lots of ice cream in the summer. "I think of food as more than just nutrition, but as great memories with people whom you love. So when I do eat out or have dessert, I try to really enjoy those moments," Viola says.

In the future, Viola hopes to enter a career in marketing while pursuing her passions for cooking and food photography. It's also her dream to open a café called "The Sunshine Eatery."

1. Why do you appreciate home cooking?

I love home cooking because I know exactly what goes into my food and I can adjust the food to my liking. For example, I enjoy spicy foods, so I can just add as much spice as I like. Also, I find the process of cooking or baking quite meditative. It's a way for me to get lost in thoughts and forget about other things. Having delicious things to eat afterwards is also definitely a plus.

2. What is the biggest influence on your cooking style?

I think the biggest influence on my cooking style would probably be my love for different cuisines and interests in different cultures. I love traveling and experiencing new foods and flavors. There is a strong influence of different Asian cuisines in my food because the flavor palette is so rich and multifaceted, and I love trying and combining different spices. Another big influence is definitely my lifestyle. Being a student or even when I was working a full-time job in the past, I always tried to pack a lot of nutrition and flavor into dishes that I could make in under fifteen minutes. Therefore, my dishes are usually very easy and quick to make while also being healthy and delicious.

3. What are your favorite dishes and why?

I love everything that uses a lot of spices and has a thick creamy sauce such as different curries or stews. One of my absolute favorite dishes would be a green Thai curry with tofu and brown rice.

4. Were there any challenges and obstacles when you learned cooking?

I think one challenge that I faced and still face is to replace normal and unhealthy ingredients while still creating something that tastes good and has the right texture. For example, some sweeteners just don't give the same sweetness that white sugar gives. It's just about experimenting and trial and error—but instead of seeing it as a challenge with a negative connotation, I truly have fun while testing different recipes.

5. What does your kitchen look like? What are your essential kitchen tools?

My kitchen is always filled with lots of jars that are filled with bulk food items, such as nuts, seeds and grains. I also always have a few tins of different beans like chickpeas or kidney beans and some frozen spinach and frozen berries in my freezer.

It's always handy to have staples like these in your kitchen for those days when you cannot be bothered or don't have the time to go shopping. My essential kitchen tools include my Vitamix blender, which is used to make smoothies, soups and things like hummus. I also have a nonstick pot that can either be used as a pan or a pot, and I do love waffles so my Belgian waffle iron is also one of my most favorite kitchen tools.

6. Could you share one occasion when your food or preparation made a marvelous impression on your family and your friends?

There was one time when I cooked a chickpea curry for my cousin, who loves meat, and he had actually been feeling quite sick the entire day but he loved my curry so much that he took on the challenge to be vegetarian for a month, and essentially lived off of my recipe for the curry during that time.

Vietnamese Summer Rolls

Makes about 6 rolls

» Ingredients

· Rice paper sheets

· 1 medium carrot, julienned or sliced into very thin strips

· 1 medium zucchini, julienned or sliced into very thin strips

· ½ mango, sliced

· 1 block of smoked tofu, sliced into strips

· Optional: a bunch of coriander/ cilantro, avocado, additional vegetables

To serve

Peanut satay sauce

· 1 tablespoon of peanut butter

· A dash of curry powder

· Splash of soy sauce

· Water

» Method

1. After preparing your vegetables, dip one rice paper sheet into warm water and transfer to a board or large plate.

2. Once the rice paper has softened a little bit, start assembling your roll: Place your carrot, zucchini, mango, tofu and whatever else you want to enjoy in your summer rolls vertically in the middle of the rice paper.

3. Fold in the top as well as the bottom side of the rice paper over the vegetables so that once they are rolled, the vegetables are secure and won't slide out.

4. Now use one side of the rice paper to fold over the filling, using your fingers to tightly roll the vegetables towards the remaining side of the rice paper.

5. Continue rolling until there are no vegetables left.

6. For the sauce, simply whisk the peanut butter, curry powder, soy sauce (to taste), and a little bit of water until creamy. Dip and enjoy!

Asian Stir-Fried Rice Noodle

Serves 2–3

» Ingredients

· 2 servings of broad rice noodles
  (about 110 g)

· 1 handful of sugar snap peas

· 1 medium carrot, julienned or
  sliced finely

· 1 cup of bean sprouts

· 1 cup of broccoli florets

· 1 block of firm tofu, cut into
  bite-sized pieces

· Soy sauce and Chinese vinegar
  to taste

· 1 tablespoon Lao Gan Ma chili
  sauce (use less if you cannot
  handle too much spice)

· 1 tablespoon of vegetable oil
  (rapeseed for example)

» Method

1 . Place your rice noodles in a bowl, boil some water in a kettle or a pot and pour the boiling water over your dry rice noodles. Stir occasionally. In the meantime, wash and prepare your vegetables and tofu.

2. Heat your oil in a wok or a deep pan and add your tofu. Once your tofu is browned on all sides, add the vegetables, starting with the broccoli and the sugar snap peas as they take longer to cook. Cook for about 2 minutes.

3. Add your carrot and bean sprouts to the wok. While the tofu and vegetables are cooking, drain your now-soft broad rice noodles and stir them into the vegetables.

4. Finally, add soy sauce, Chinese vinegar to taste and the Lao Gan Ma chili sauce and mix everything well. Cook for another minute before serving.

Malin Nilsson

Blog/ **Good Eatings**

*"In my book, the best spice is
a little bit of love."*

Malin Nilsson is the writer and creator behind the food blog "Good Eatings," where she shares whole food vegan recipes, city guides from her travels, and tips for a vegan lifestyle. She currently lives in the Swedish countryside with her boyfriend Rob.

The Kitchen Is My Stage

Outside a rural village in Sweden's most southern county, Skåne, dwell Malin Nilsson and her boyfriend Rob. Malin, a foodie since a young girl, shares her vegan recipes on "Good Eatings," the name of both a blog and a YouTube channel. Rob, on the other hand, excels at videography, filming and helping with post-production. With one being a creative director and the other being a technical expert, the couple are not only companions to each other in daily life, but also good teammates. Besides working together on Malin's platform, they also handle corporate communication projects.

The house where they live is situated amid a wide field, with breathtaking scenery, especially during the wintertime when everywhere is white, crisp and clear. The couple find peace in this small corner of the world and live a simple yet adventurous life. Along with maintaining her blog, Malin is studying to become a health coach. The majority of her time is dedicated to learning about nutrition and health practices and doing assignments. Usually when she finishes a day's tasks, she walks around the village to get some fresh air and returns home to cook dinner with Rob. There are forests nearby for nice walks and if they travel a little farther, there are beautiful hiking opportunities along the coastline.

Being vegan and vegetarian, the couple consume mainly unrefined grains, pulses, legumes, vegetables, fruits, nuts and seeds. They have a small garden outside their house where they occasionally grow vegetables like beets, carrots, radishes and pumpkins. For daily produce, they visit the village convenience store, or travel at least once a week to a nearby town to visit the supermarket where they get specialty food and herbs; for bulk items like grains and beans they visit another bulk food store which is an hour's drive from home. Although grocery shopping is time-consuming, it is how they live more intentionally and plan their meals better.

Before settling down in this rural house in Sweden, the couple lived in London for a few years. At that time, Malin was planning to pursue her dream of becoming a professional contemporary dancer, but after a serious injury and a heartbreaking period, she decided to gather herself up and redirect her interest. Because of her indigestion problem, Malin started doing research on food and health. At the same time, moving in with Rob, who had been a vegetarian for more than ten years, greatly influenced Malin's diet. She not only learned a lot of new recipes, but also treated the food she ate in a whole new way, from a more ethical point of view. Eventually she decided to go vegan, first with only her food choices, but gradually integrating veganism fully into her lifestyle.

"After changing my diet, I felt a million times better and I was seeing a lot of health benefits. My wellbeing just

reached a new level which I was so excited about," Malin says. She was also surprised to find that eliminating meat and dairy didn't mean there were fewer possibilities for cooking. For example, she could add in many colors, textures and flavors with plants and prepare her food in a variety of ways: raw, sauteed, flash-fried, slow-cooked, baked, soaked, pickled, etc.

The kitchen has become the home court for Malin: she cooks, tests the recipes, films and photographs. It is also her stage when she wants to dance around. Although she may not be followed by a spotlight, the kitchen is the place where Malin makes herself shine.

1. After your injury, why did you decide to redirect your attention to food?

I have always loved food—my parents will vouch for that. I used to be the kid who ate cabbage leaves in the shopping cart. My grandmother used to let me eat butter with a spoon out of the carton. I'd even eat pepper out of the shaker and once I ate a whole *monstera* leaf from the pot in our living room before my mother caught me. I almost scared her to death doing that but luckily I chose a plant that is not poisonous! It's safe to say I've had a love affair with eating food for a long time. And as I grew a little older, I enjoyed learning new recipes and about different cultures' food traditions but it wasn't until I felt the connection between food and health and as a way of choosing not to harm other beings that I became passionate about doing research, being creative with food and sharing it with others online.

2. Was it difficult for you to make the transition to be a vegan?

No, it wasn't. Although when you begin to change your lifestyle it can be quite daunting as you have to do some research and learn new things, but the one thing I think people find most difficult is being different from others, especially in relation to family and friends. Eating differently and researching recipes, hygiene, cleaning products, clothing and shoe brands etc. is easy—you just need to take the time, but other people's reactions to you making changes is something that is harder to affect.

Personally, I was able to do it in a very understanding and supportive environment and the negative reactions I got more or less washed off rather quickly. I was convinced this was the right thing to do for me and there's never anything wrong with choosing to do less harm in this world, which I still think is true. If there's something you believe in, which overall has a net worth of good, I think it's worth the hardship. And at the end of the day when you've gotten through those first moments where you're not quite sure how to work it all out, and when you've made it clear to others that this is not just a phase, then it's smooth sailing.

3. What is your culinary philosophy?

I'd say my culinary philosophy is all about making the most out of plants and cooking from the heart. In general I like to roll with the seasons, but find comfort in some classic recipes using non-seasonal ingredients here and there. And for me, cooking should be fun and done with curiosity. There are lots of things to discover in your own kitchen through cooking, about food for sure but also about cultures and your own creativity.

4. From where do you draw inspiration for your recipes?

I draw inspiration from what's in season, from traveling or other food experiences, from other creatives on the internet, and sometimes even from an empty fridge combined with needing to make some dinner. It can be a color, a texture, a combination of flavors or just a random meal that sparks the idea for a new recipe. Being open and curious is the best way to fuel your creativity.

5. In your opinion, what is the trend now in home cooking?

I definitely think we've been seeing that plant-based cooking has been trending for a while and I think it will continue to do so. Other than that, it seems meal prepping has become a real trend where people want to make sure they stay on top of their preferred eating habits and find ways to prepare their food ahead of time to make sure they do. It might not be the most exciting trend, but I think it's definitely a good thing and I'm glad something that helps so many people stick to their intentions is being widely shared.

Peanut Butter Hot Pot with Winter Vegetables and Chickpeas

Serves 4–6

» Ingredients

Hot pot

· 1 large brown onion, peeled and in 8 rough pieces

· 5 garlic cloves, peeled

· 1 inch ginger, peeled and very roughly chopped

· 1 teaspoon hot chili flakes, or less/more depending on your preference

· 1 teaspoon paprika powder

· ¾ teaspoon ground turmeric

· ¾ teaspoon cumin

· 1 can (400 ml) chopped tomatoes

· 1 cup unsweetened plant milk (Malin uses soy or oat)

· ½ cup water

· ½ cup smooth peanut butter

· 1 tablespoon vegetable stock powder, or one cube

· 1 tablespoon coconut sugar

· 1 small cauliflower, in florets

· ½ small sweet pumpkin, in bite-sized cubes

· 5 large Swiss chard leaves, stems removed and leafy parts in rough pieces

· 1 can chickpeas, drained and rinsed

· Sea salt and black pepper, to taste

To serve

· Brown rice

· Sesame seeds

· Quick pickles

· Spring onion

· Salted peanuts

· Lime wedges

» Method

1. Start by blitzing your onion, garlic and ginger together with your spices (except for salt and pepper) in a food processor for a couple of minutes. You should have a rough (i.e. not completely smooth) paste.

2. Add a little oil to a sauce pan over medium heat and sauté the paste for a minute or two until very fragrant.

3. Then add your plant milk, water, peanut butter, vegetable stock powder and coconut sugar. Bring to a simmer and stir to combine into an almost-smooth sauce. Let simmer for 2 to 3 minutes to let the flavors meld together.

4. Finally add your chopped tomatoes and vegetables, except for chard, and simmer covered for 15 minutes or until your vegetables are tender.

5. Add your chard and chickpeas, stir to combine and let simmer another couple of minutes until the chard is wilted and chickpeas warm.

6. Serve with brown rice studded with sesame seeds, quick pickles (Malin uses carrots), spring onion, salted peanuts and lime wedges to squeeze on top.

Tofu Bánh mì with Sriracha Cashew Mayo

» Ingredients

Smoky tofu

· ½ pound (270 g) block of firm tofu, excess water pressed out and cut into 8 slices

· ⅓ cup soy sauce

· 2 tablespoons rice vinegar

· 1 ½ tablespoons maple syrup

· 1 tablespoon molasses, optional

· 1 tablespoon liquid smoke

· 2 teaspoons Sriracha sauce

· Black pepper, to taste

Radish & carrot pickle

· 1 ¼ cups carrot, julienned

· ¾ cup radish, sliced

· ⅓ cup rice vinegar

· ⅓ cup warm water

· 2 tablespoons maple syrup

· 1 garlic clove, finely sliced

· 8 peppercorns

· ½ teaspoon salt

Sriracha cashew mayo

· 1 cup cashews, soaked overnight or for 30 minutes in hot water

· 1 garlic clove, roughly chopped

· 1 medium-sized lemon, juice only

· 1 tablespoon Sriracha sauce

· 1 tablespoon apple cider vinegar

· ½ teaspoon ground mustard, optional but ideal

· ¼ teaspoon sea salt

· ¼ cup water, or more to reach preferred consistency

To serve

· 2 baguettes, gluten-free if required

· ⅓ cucumber, mandolined into ribbons or sliced

· 2 spring onions, sliced

· A handful of fresh coriander (cilantro)

· 4 handfuls of your favorite lettuce or green leaves

» Method

Tofu

1. Mix all the marinade ingredients in a shallow bowl. Then immerse the tofu in the sauce, making sure it's all or mainly covered, and then cover it with a plate and a small weight (like a jam jar) to make sure the tofu stays covered. Set aside in the fridge overnight or at least an hour before cooking.

2. When you are ready to cook it, heat a griddle or frying pan to medium heat. Lightly oil the pan, if needed, using a paper towel to prevent sticking. Grill/fry your tofu for 3 to 4 minutes on the first side and roughly 2 on the other.

Radish & carrot quick pickle

3. Mix all the wet ingredients as well as peppercorns, salt and garlic in a jar. When the sweetener is dissolved, add your vegetables to the jar and leave in the fridge overnight or at least one hour before assembling the baguette.

Sriracha cashew mayo

4. Place all the ingredients in a high-speed blender or food processor and blend until smooth and creamy. Adjust the seasoning to suit your preference.

Assembling your Vietnamese baguette

5. If the baguette is not fresh from the baker, you can toast it slightly in the oven, but this is optional. Then cut the baguette in half and slice it open but not all the way through.

6. Slather some cashew mayo on both sides and layer the green leaves, cucumber ribbons, pickled radish and carrot, tofu and top it all off with spring onion and fresh coriander.

Lore Salas

Brand/ **Dates and Avocados**

"My main goal is to help people dive into the joy of sweets while nourishing their bodies."

Lore Salas is the founder of "Dates and Avocados," a brand that wishes to spread the idea of plant-based baking. Originally from Spain, she now works as a recipe consultant and travels around the world.

Healthy Desserts:
Gifts for the Sweet Tooth

It seems to be a universal phenomenon that people don't relate "health" with "pleasure." Many people have bad feelings after they enjoy a delicious dessert and count how many miles they have to run to lose the weight. After three years of researching and experimenting with plant-based baking, Lore Salas wishes to become the force standing between "health" and "pleasure," pulling them towards the center and bringing them into the same dish.

Lore was born in the north of Spain, but spent most of her adolescence in Barcelona, which is the city she feels most attached to. Her dad's family has a rich cooking background and there was always a feast when they went to her aunt's house for lunch. For Lore, her aunt's kitchen was just like a playground, full of different dishes cooking at the same time. She remembers helping her aunt take care of the pots and stir the stews. Her grandma, who has lived with her aunt, is the permanent assistant in the kitchen, washing and peeling vegetables or preparing Spanish specialties like *ensaladilla rusa* (potato salad) or *macedonia de frutas* (fruit salad).

Since she was a kid, Lore has had a passion for art and a talent for numbers. She studied civil engineering in university and later worked as a math teacher for several years. In 2015, she moved to the US because of her husband's job location. This was the time when Lore started to reexamine her career and her life. Following

her internal calling to reconnect with food, she enrolled in the pastry program of Houston Community College. Although she had a sweet tooth, she couldn't enjoy herself at first. Every recipe they worked with was loaded with huge quantities of refined sugars, flours and butter. This was very frustrating to Lore because she was obsessed with healthy eating at that time. Seeing her struggle, one of her instructors, Chef Eddy Van Damme (co-author of the well-known culinary textbook *On Baking*) encouraged her to come up with new alternatives for ingredients.

The rest of the semester witnessed Lore testing different kinds of natural sweeteners. She has discovered dates as an alternative to sugar, and avocado instead of butter. New paths started to appear and Lore was pleased to find out that she could finally create the food she could happily devour. Those months in the pastry school were a huge test for her, yet they set the path she is still following to this day.

Following her studies in pastry school, she continued to learn plant-based cooking at Matthew Kenney Culinary. This was the time when the idea of establishing her own brand, "Dates and Avocados," started to take root. Her wish was to inspire others to try plant-based baking and create the desserts that everyone can enjoy, without guilty feelings.

Over the past two years, Dates and Avocados has grown from an Instagram account to a website and now an energetic start-up company. Lore now works as a consultant for restaurants and cafés around the world. Because of her profession and her husband's job location, Lore travels a lot. Wherever she moves, she will always find a proper kitchen where she can work. She brings along her blender, food processor, cake tins, molds and essential props, which occupy two suitcases. Creating recipes and taking photos in constantly changing kitchens are her biggest challenge, but Lore says this also makes her continuously push her improvization and creativity to another level.

"My biggest accomplishment has been building my own company in the middle of all this chaos," Lore says. "As a student, I never would have dreamed I'd end up as a professional consultant developing recipes for restaurants in so many countries, writing a cookbook, and teaching and connecting with so many passionate foodies around the world. It really is a dream coming true."

1. Why are you interested in creating healthy desserts? What's your secret to making them healthy instead of heavy and sweet?

At the beginning it was something personal. My last college years counted as some of my most unhealthy times. I was running and exercising often, but I also started eating junk food, going out late and sleeping too few hours. It was a life dedicated to studying and indulging myself. After college, I traveled around the country studying and exploring. Looking to disrupt the unhealthy patterns I'd developed—as well as to reconnect with my creative roots—I moved to the United States and then enrolled in the pastry school in Houston. For me it was a matter of health to find a way of enjoying my sweet tooth, but at the same time eating as healthily as possible.

On the other hand, I wouldn't say there's any particular secret. It boils down to hours of experimentation. In the beginning, I used to think that with just exchanging one ingredient for another, I could get the same results and slightly similar taste, but that's almost never the case. The truth is that most of the times I had to rethink the recipe, trying to achieve the same results with different ingredients. That eventually lead me to create new and completely different recipes that are not trying to imitate anything. That is where I think my work is moving.

2. How do you keep yourself inspired and motivated with recipe development?

I'm continuously checking recipes in books and blogs. I love to read the ingredients list and observe the colors and textures in the pictures. I consider myself a perfectionist, and the tiniest details always catch my attention. Besides books, what inspire me the most to create new recipes are ingredients. I go to the farmers' markets and try seasonal fruits, smell the herbs, see the flowers—nothing is more inspiring than that. I really struggle when I don't have access to fresh local ingredients. I do not like buying in big supermarkets where food comes canned and in plastic packages. So if you manage to learn how to keep youself inspired, then what you need is motivation to work. Personally, food has become the way I channel my creativity and passion for art, so I am constantly going back to recipe development and food because that is the best way to express myself.

3. After two years in the US, you moved to Shanghai and spent a year in China. Chinese food is very different from Western cuisine. Was there any food-related "culture shock?"

For a person with a plant-based diet, it was kind of shocking to realize the amount of meat that was used in Chinese dishes, and how difficult it was for me to make myself understood when I was asking for vegetarian food. But that was just in the beginning—as time passed by, I was able to immerse myself into Chinese gastronomy and discover how rich this cuisine really is. I got some of the best culinary experiences of my life in China. For example, at the Chinese restaurant Fu He Hui, in Shanghai, vegetarian food is taken to another level. There are also so many ingredients and techniques that I learned in the course of my time in China that have been very useful, which I add to my personal recipes.

4. You established your brand "Dates and Avocados" last year and traveled around the world, working as a consultant for restaurants and cafés. What are your expectations for the future?

I want to learn—that is my main priority. You won't believe how many incredible chefs, bakers, and pastry chefs there are around the world who are open to sharing what they do and how they do it. More and more people are deciding to eat consciously, meaning they want to know what they eat, where it comes from and how it is prepared. As chefs and restaurant owners, we have the responsibility of going the extra mile to bring exciting, conscious, delicious food to everybody. My expectations are basically sharing everything I know and everything I am learning, whether it's through books, courses, workshops, consulting etc., and spread the word so we can keep empowering people to learn how to eat the way they want to.

Eventually I'd love to use all this knowledge to open a café or restaurant where, instead of just sharing recipes or procedures on how to make something, I could make sure people can enjoy this nourishing, healthy and delicious food in the best environment and with the best culinary experience possible.

10-Minute Vegan Miso Soup

» Ingredients

- 4 cups filtered water, plus some more for rehydrating wakame (Undaria pinnatifida)
- 2 pieces of dry kombu seaweed (about 4" x 2", or 10 cm x 5 cm)
- 1 tablespoon dry wakame seaweed
- 2 to 3 tablespoons chickpea miso paste
- 1 tablespoon tamari (or soy) sauce
- Salt and fresh ground black pepper to taste
- ¼ block soft tofu, cubed into ½" cubes
- 2 shiitake mushrooms, finely sliced
- Enoki mushrooms, as many as desired
- 1 okra, finely sliced
- 1 teaspoon chives, finely chopped
- Fresh herbs such as nasturtiums, mustard leaves, etc.

» Method

1. Start rehydrating the dried wakame with water in a bowl. Let stand about 15 minutes, then drain using a strainer. You will notice the volume has increased considerably.

2. Heat 4 cups of water in a pot over low heat. Add kombu and cook until the water just begins to simmer. Remove from heat, strain the seaweed, and set the broth aside.

3. Remove one cup of this broth and whisk in the miso paste. Pour this mixture back into the pot, stir well, and add the tamari sauce.

4. Add the tofu cubes, mushrooms and wakame, and cook at low heat for another 2 minutes or so.

5. Serve in a bowl and garnish with the okra "stars," chives, and herbs.

Hazelnut & Blueberry Cookies

» Ingredients

Dry ingredients

· 1 cup almond flour

· ¾ cup rolled oats

· ¼ cup shredded coconut

· ¼ cup hazelnuts, chopped

· 2 tablespoons flax meal

· 1 teaspoon baking powder

· ½ teaspoon vanilla bean, seeded (can be substituted by ½ teaspoon vanilla extract)

· ¼ teaspoon cinnamon

· ¼ teaspoon pink Himalayan salt

Wet ingredients

· 5 medjool dates, pitted and chopped

· ¼ cup almond milk

· 1 banana, overripe

· 3 tablespoons almond butter

· 3 tablespoons coconut oil

· ½ cup frozen blueberries

» Method

1. Start mixing flax meal with almond milk. Whisk until well-incorporated and set aside while preparing the rest of the ingredients.

2. In a large bowl, combine dry ingredients together and mix well using a spatula or whisk.

3. In the jar of a blender, blend the dates with the almond butter, banana, and coconut oil. Pour over a bowl and incorporate the flax mixture.

4. Progressively add wet ingredients over the bowl with dry ingredients and mix well using your hands (the mixture is very sticky, so use gloves) until a compact ball is formed.

5. Fold in the blueberries.

6. Let the mixture rest in the fridge for at least 30 minutes to set.

7. Preheat oven to 350°F (175°C).

8. Use a medium cookie scoop (size 30: 1 ounce) to scoop uniform size cookies over a baking pan lined with parchment paper.

9. Flatten the balls slightly with your fingers and add a few extra chocolate pieces over each cookie.

10. Bake for 17 minutes. Increase the temperature of the oven to 375°F (190°C) and bake for another 3 to 4 minutes until the sides are golden brown. Make sure you don't overbake them.

11. Remove from the oven and let cool.

12. Store in glass airtight containers up to 3 days.

Kati Boden

"I love living in various countries. I'm a curious person and I soak up every little aspect of a place, from politics to fashion to what people eat."

Kati Boden is the author behind the food blog "black.white.vivid." As a world traveler, she enjoys living a nomadic life, indulging herself in cooking and photography.

A Kitchen of the Delicious World

Kati Boden, a lover of the nomadic life, is constantly on the move. Originally from Germany, she has lived and visited more than seventy countries. With every place she goes, she devours the local flavor and introduces the flavors to her own kitchen. In one category of her blog "black.white.vivid," her readers' taste buds are taken on a trip around the world: French pear and apple galette with rosemary syrup, Lebanese *za'atar man'oushe* buns, and Emirati saffron cardamom pancakes, to name just a few.

At the beginning of 2018, Katie moved to Dubai with her partner, embarking on another unexpected adventure. To her surprise, the vibe is very multicultural in Dubai, with very talented and ambitious people living there, thriving for change. "Every culture brings in their food, way of cooking, culinary expertise and they combine it with what's around them. So you end up with an interesting mix of flavors, cuisines and fashions," says Katie. So far, life is very easy and enjoyable. You can see her posting photos from her seat on the breathtaking sand dunes, holding a plate of mouthwatering Emirati sweet dumplings.

"I was born in the former GDR where we basically lived behind a wall and traveling was not possible or very restricted. So when the Berlin Wall fell I guess my parents wanted to make up for their and my missed opportunities of visiting new countries and cultures," Kati says. At the age of six, she went abroad by herself for the first time, joining a holiday camp in Poland. By the time she graduated from high school, she had seen most of Europe and some parts of North America. As a young adult, she earned her Bachelor's degree and two Master's degrees in Marketing and Management, respectively in the Netherlands, the UK, and France. After that, she returned to Germany where she worked at Amazon for two years, and since then she has lived in Hong Kong, Cairo, Istanbul and now Dubai.

It was during her travels when she began to feel passionate about cooking. When she moved to Cairo, she realized that a lot of her favorite things like almond milk, cashew butter, and plant-based yogurt were not available, so she started making these things at home and has continued her culinary journey ever since.

Traveling has become her biggest source of inspiration for the recipes. She rarely cooks in her accommodations when she travels because she doesn't want to miss out on the local food, but when she returns home, she will re-create the food in her own way. As she mostly eats a plant-based diet, the vegetarian dishes she encounters during her travels become her beloved food.

One of her all-time favorite recipes is whole roasted

cauliflower, which was inspired by her travels to Israel with an old friend. Late one night at a Tel Aviv restaurant, they randomly picked some vegetable dishes from the menu, but the servings turned out to be more than satisfying, especially one dish with cauliflower. "It was buttery inside, crispy and slightly burned on the outside, served with a tahini dressing and topped with crunchy pomegranate seeds and fresh parsley. It was a flavor explosion," Kati recalls. It was so good that Kati re-creates this recipe at home regularly, and has won the approval of friends and family.

Along with cooking, Kati is also enthusiastic about photography. Through constant practice, she has learned to tell a story with light, no matter if it's the warm desert light at sunset, Nordic moody light or harsh summer light shining through the window. Every time she plans a shoot, she tries to imagine the feeling she wants to communicate with her photos. She puts herself into that scene and lets her thoughts run free.

"They say you are a creative person or an analytical person. I truly enjoy both sides." After being in the marketing industry for many years, Kati started working for herself full-time in 2018. Having her own business allows her to spend time doing a lot of technical and analytical things as well as creative and emotional tasks.

1. Are you a self-taught cook? What obstacles have you met when practicing cookery?

I think the reason it took me so long to get into cooking was because I always thought that you had to learn how to cook with cookbooks or in culinary school. So I would buy all these cookbooks because I liked the idea of becoming a better home cook. But most cookbooks tell you indeed how to cook, step-by-step, but they don't tell you why they do it the way they do. I always found this very frustrating.

When I moved to Egypt, I was forced to read recipes but once I started to understand a few things about cooking I experimented a lot. I was often inspired by foods I had seen or eaten on my travels. As I mostly cook plant-based food at home, I veganized many of the recipes. For most of the foods I tried out at home, there are no recipes out there because these dishes are not so well-known, so consequently vegan recipes are even rarer. However, even though it was hard to get into the habit of cooking, it wasn't the biggest obstacle. I'm not a very patient person when it comes to cooking. And by that I mean that I

don't like making a recipe ten times before I finally make a perfect version of it. So I started investing in cookbooks that teach you how to cook rather than what to cook.

2. Could you give examples of how you keep a balanced and healthy life, especially with regard to your eating and cooking habits?

I love trying out new foods and dishes. That way I automatically try out new ingredients every now and then. I also love to cook all kinds of recipes from all over the world. So at home I cook Thai food one day and Mexican-inspired food the next day. But no matter if I make spaghetti or Turkish flatbread, I always serve a portion of salad with it. Even when I go out for dinner, I usually order a side salad with my food. It simply helps to get in some greens first before you indulge on carbs. And carbs are an essential part of your diet, too. But everything comes in moderation.

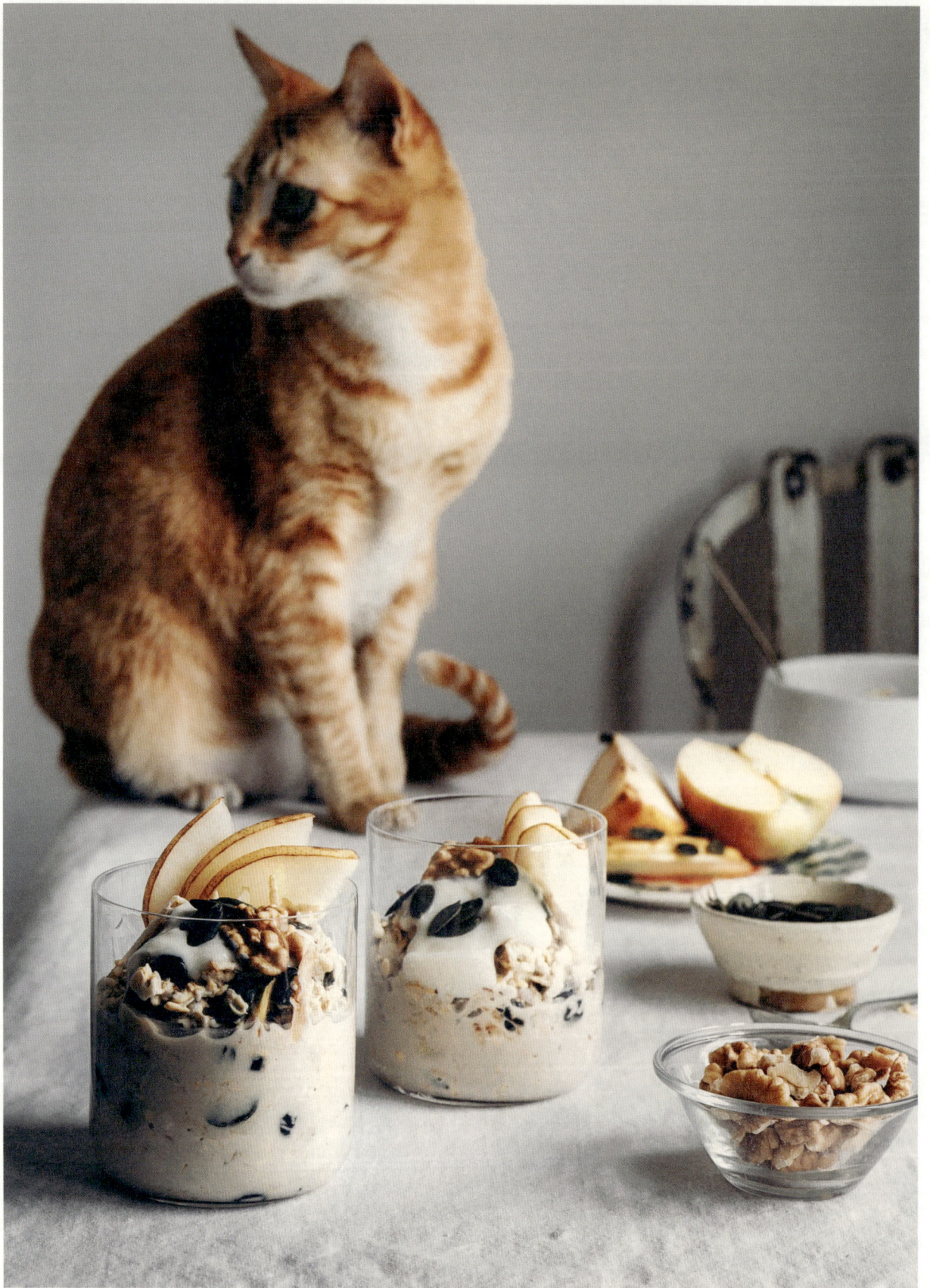

3. Besides being a lover of food and traveling, you are also a talented photographer. I'm enthralled every time I look at your atmospheric photos, so I'm curious to know your magic: How do you tell a story within a photo through food styling and light?

My photography journey was very similar to my cooking journey. It has evolved over the years. As with cooking, I always had the ambition to become better at it, so I also experimented a lot. Especially in the beginning I took an endless number of photos, each and every single day. Finding my style didn't happen overnight. It's still a work in progress but there is one element that has always inspired me, and that is light. Mastering light helped me to find my style. I've always been intrigued by photos that tell a story with light. Sometimes I look at a simple image, of perhaps a glass of wine, and the contrast between shadow and light makes me feel like it's the most complex piece of art. Light is my muse and it's the one thing that inspires me the most.

Food styling is certainly an important aspect, too. I had to learn that merely placing a kitchen towel next to a bowl doesn't tell much of a story. So when I plan a shoot I try to imagine the feeling and vibe I want to communicate with my photo. I turn on some suitable music and let my thoughts run free. I really feel that mentally putting yourself into a scene helps to create a better photograph. I think about all things associated with the food I want to photograph. Like how did I prepare it and can I use some elements of that in my photo? For example, when I baked a lemon cake, why not show a squeezed-out lemon or the lemon zester? Or how would a perfect food scene look when I enjoy it as an afternoon treat? I'd definitely have a cup of tea with it, maybe reading a book while the sun is warming my face. It's more about portraying a feeling than simply showing a recipe.

Whole Roasted Cauliflower

Serves 4

» Ingredients

· 1 whole medium-sized head of
  cauliflower covered in green
  leaves
· 3 tablespoons olive oil
· Good-quality sea salt
· 3 tablespoons tahini
· 3 tablespoons vegan yogurt (for
  example soy yogurt)
· ½ lemon
· 1 handful of flat parsley, chopped
· 2 to 3 tablespoons pomegranate
  seeds
· Salt & pepper to taste

» Method

1. Preheat the oven to 430°F (220°C).

2. Place cauliflower in a metal pot and fill three-quarters of it with water. Add ½ tablespoon (10 g) salt per liter of water (this might sound like a lot, but it makes all the difference). Cover with lid, bring to boil and then lower the heat to medium and continue to boil for 10 minutes. Drain it.

3. Either brush the cauliflower with olive oil or put some of the oil on your hands and rub the cauliflower. Sprinkle with a little salt.

4. Place cauliflower on a baking dish and bake until the top turns golden. Katie likes to keep it in the oven a little longer so the crust is really crispy and almost dark brown (some spots even burned) for even better taste.

5. In the meantime, mix tahini, vegan yogurt, lemon juice from ½ lemon, some salt and pepper. Adjust to taste by adding more tahini or lemon juice if you like.

6. Drizzle tahini sauce on top of cauliflower and sprinkle with pomegranate seeds and chopped parsley leaves.

7. Serve warm (though this dish tastes amazing lukewarm and even cold) as a starter or with other appetizers and bread as a main dish.

Vegan Savory Babka with Coriander, Basil and Sour Cashew Cream

Cashew sour cream

· 1 cup soaked cashews (soak at least 30 minutes in hot water or overnight in cold water)

· ½ cup water

· ½ lemon, juice

· 2 teaspoons apple cider vinegar

· ½ teaspoon salt

· 2 handfuls basil leaves

· 2 handfuls coriander leaves (cilantro)

Dough

· 1 ¼ cups (280 ml) water

· 2 ½ teaspoons active dry yeast

· 2 teaspoons coconut sugar (or any other sugar)

· ¼ cup (60 ml) grapeseed oil or any other neutral-flavored oil

· 2 cups (150 g) spelt flour

· 2 cups (150 g) wheat flour

· 2 teaspoons salt

Glazing

· 1 ½ teaspoons pure maple syrup or any other syrup or honey

· 1 ½ teaspoons olive oil

» Method

Cashew sour cream

1. Add soaked cashews, lemon juice, salt and apple cider vinegar to blender. Gradually start adding water, first ¼ cup and more if needed to make a smooth but solid cream. You want a cream-cheese-like consistency, not too liquid but also not too coarse. Put in the fridge as it will thicken further with time.

Dough

1. Start by mixing lukewarm water with sugar in a large bowl. Sprinkle with yeast. Set aside and wait for 10 minutes or until you see some foam on the surface. That means your yeast is activated and ready to go.

2. Mix in spelt and wheat flour, oil and salt to the yeast mixture. Mix well with a wooden spoon and knead everything into a shaggy dough. Add up to ½ cup of flour if the dough is still very wet and sticky.

3. On a lightly floured surface knead dough for 5 to 7 minutes. Knead until it is smooth.

4. Grease the inside of the bowl with a little bit of oil.

5. Form a ball, put it back into the bowl, cover with a damp kitchen towel and put it in a warm place for at least 1.5 hours, preferably 2 hours.

6. Once the dough has at least doubled in size, punch the dough down.

7. Lightly grease one loaf pan (10" or 26 cm long) or line it with parchment paper.

8. Place dough on a lightly floured surface and roll out to a rectangle and orient so a short side is facing you. The short side should be 1.5 x the length of your loaf pan.

9. Spread sour cashew cream over dough to extend to the edges. Sprinkle with herbs.

10. Slowly roll up dough away from you. This will get a little messy.

11. Lift up rolled, filled dough and twist it gently once. Fold in half and place it into your prepared loaf pan. Cover with damp kitchen towel and let it rest for 1 hour.

12. Preheat oven to 350°F (175°C) 30 minutes after the second rise starts.

13. Whisk together the maple syrup and oil in a small bowl. Brush the top of the babka with the glazing.

14. Bake for 35 to 45 minutes or until the crust is golden brown. Cool the pan for 5 to 10 minutes before you take it out. Let it cool on the cooling rack.

15. Eat the same day or the day after or freeze slices of the babka for up to one month. Serve with avocado, olive oil and sea salt or eat them just plain.

INDEX

Unless otherwise stated, all the photos are credited to the contributors.

Kathrin Salzwedel

Instagram @klaraslife
http://klaraslife.com
P172-P187

Kati Boden

Instagram @blackwhitevivid
http://blackwhitevivid.com
P232-P248

Lore Salas

Instagram @datesandavocados
http://datesandavocados.com
P216-P231

Lydia Wong

Instagram @gingerandchorizo
https://gingerandchorizo.wordpress.com
P158-P171

Maggie Zhu

Instagram @omnivorescookbook
https://omnivorescookbook.com
P080-P095

Malin Nilsson

Instagram @goodeatings
http://goodeatings.com
P200-P215

Katie Brigstock & Safia Shakarchi

Instagram @wearecookandbaker
https://www.wearecookandbaker.com
Photography: Ellie Edkins (p028, p032-034, p036-037),
Holly Wulff Petersen (p029, p031, p040-041),
Safia Shakarchi (p035, p039, p043-044)
P028-P045

Meg van der Kruik

Instagram @thismessisours
https://thismessisours.com
Photo on p147 by Emma K. Morris
P144-P157

Melissa Ofoedu

Instagram @asweetpointofview
https://www.sweetpointofview.com
P112-P125

Samantha Woods

Instagram @thebotanicalkitchen
http://thebotanicalkitchen.com
P046-P063

Silvia Bifaro

Instagram @silvia_salvialimone
http://www.salvialimone.com
P126-P143

Viola Hou

Instagram @thesunshineeatery
https://www.youtube.com/thesunshineeatery
P188-P199

Acknowledgements

We would like to express our gratitude to all of the bloggers, photographers and stylists for their generous contributions of images and interview answers. We are also very grateful to many other people whose names do not appear in the credits but who made specific contributions and provided support. Without them, the successful completion of this book would not be possible. Special thanks to all of the contributors for sharing their innovation and creativity with our readers around the world.